Cake on Tuesday

25 LESSONS TO UNLOCK
CORPORATE INNOVATION

Cake on
Tuesday

ELIZABETH BIENIEK

Advantage | Books

Published by Advantage Books, Charleston, South Carolina.
An imprint of Advantage Media.

ADVANTAGE is a registered trademark, and the Advantage colophon is a trademark of Advantage Media Group, Inc.

Printed in the United States of America.

10 9 8 7 6 5 4 3 2 1

ISBN: 979-8-89188-040-5 (Paperback)
ISBN: 979-8-89188-111-2 (Hardcover)
ISBN: 979-8-89188-042-9 (eBook)

Library of Congress Control Number: 2024904913

Cover design by Analisa Smith.
Layout design by Matthew Morse.

This publication is designed to provide accurate and authoritative information in regard to the subject matter covered. It is sold with the understanding that the publisher is not engaged in rendering legal, accounting, or other professional services. If legal advice or other expert assistance is required, the services of a competent professional person should be sought.

Advantage Books is an imprint of Advantage Media Group. Advantage Media helps busy entrepreneurs, CEOs, and leaders write and publish a book to grow their business and become the authority in their field. Advantage authors comprise an exclusive community of industry professionals, idea-makers, and thought leaders. For more information go to **advantagemedia.com**.

Contents

Foreword

"OMG!"

That was my reaction when I saw the first demo of Webex Hologram, the output of a four-month innovation effort I had sponsored Elizabeth and team to run. The technology was impressive, but what was more impressive was that, in just fifteen weeks, after being given a small, mismatched group of "on loan" resources across the globe, Elizabeth had somehow transformed them into a cohesive team running at a sprint to build something the industry had never seen before.

When Elizabeth and team first proposed we focus on the augmented and virtual reality space, I was leading Cisco's Collaboration business. This was still a nascent market, adjacent to our core business, with little direction and a lot of potential. I green-lit Elizabeth to further explore this space with a small tiger team to test technical viability and asked them to come back with a next-level proposal of how we could enter this space.

When they pitched a project plan in response, I was impressed with how clearly a road map they laid out, considering how many unknowns there still were in this space. It covered risks, opportunities, and outputs from the tiger team that precisely depicted the technology problem we were trying to solve, a minimum viable first step to a multiphase solution, and a long-term road map of where we could go. Elizabeth had identified the team she wanted, replete with names and faces in many cases, and identified skill set gaps needed for other areas. We hadn't discussed who would lead this project, but she proposed herself as the project lead with total confidence and no apparent qualms about the fact that we were venturing into uncharted waters.

As someone who's built a career leading large, multifaceted organizations, I'm always weighing the balance between meeting short-term milestones and swinging for the fences on long-term bets. The hardest part of gambling on future solutions is dealing with the ambiguity of a continually evolving plan when you never have all the pieces to the equation, and the pieces you do have keep changing. You need a certain kind of person to lead in ambiguity—not only to cast a vision but to define a path toward that vision and convince people to come along on the adventure.

The swirling cloud of questions and uncertainty around this technology exploration didn't seem to faze Elizabeth. She calmly laid out a plan that was not only logical but starkly simplistic compared to the complexity of the technology the team would be building. So, I decided to take a chance on her leadership for that first phase of the project. And then the next. And the next.

Sometimes, to go someplace new you need a different kind of leader than what brought you to where you currently are. That "something different" is what I saw in Elizabeth, and I'm glad several years ago I took that gamble.

In this book, Elizabeth reveals the other side of that journey—her leadership journey, including the steps she took to dream, discover, and build an innovative breakthrough. She also explains how she convinced an organization to fund her, a team to follow her, and me to believe in her; and she provides an inside look at the mental journey and learnings throughout that process.

If you want an unfiltered look at the making of an intrapreneur, read on. You'll enjoy the ride.

—Rowan Trollope
CEO, REDIS

Acknowledgments

"Praise God, from whom all blessings flow;
Praise Him, all creatures here below;
Praise Him above, ye heav'nly host;
Praise Father, Son, and Holy Ghost."[1]

Thank you to my sounding board, adventure buddy, and partner in all things, Nathaniel—for not only the daily hand-ground cup of coffee, adorned with freshly grated nutmeg, delivered faithfully to me every morning (to the envy of *so* many colleagues on the other side of my video calls!) but also for everything else along the way. I couldn't be me if you weren't you. I love you.

Thank you to my huckleberry, Ashley; you have gone with me into the fire again and again, and I couldn't have done this without you.

Thank you, Jim, for the opportunity and the push, Phil for all the collaboration to bring an idea to proposal, Cullen for all the technical rigor, and Rowan for sponsoring us to get off the ground.

Thank you to the amazing Gallia team that put up with all my crazy shenanigans in those early days, met every challenge with a "whatever it takes" attitude, and defied the odds to build the impossible. Y'all have a special place in my heart.

Thank you to the sponsors, the reviewers, the supporters, and those who took up the charge to usher Gallia into the Webex Hologram era.

Thank you to everyone who reviewed, edited, offered encouragement, and pushed me along the way in the creation of this book.

Introduction

My name is Elizabeth Bieniek. I've had several lengthy and largely meaningless titles made up of big words with bigger connotations, like "innovator," "intrapreneur," and "boss lady." OK, that last one might not be on a business card. But big titles don't always convey meaning well. I like simplicity. So I'm going to tell you a story. A simple story. A story in my own words. *My* story.

For the last ... goodish while, I've been employed within the realm of enterprise collaboration—that's the fancy word for the hardware and software technology companies pay a lot of money for so their employees and customers can talk to each other and among themselves. But I don't really care about the technology. This might sound a little funny considering I was part of the CTO, or chief technology office, but it's true. The technology itself is meaningless. I care about people. People have been around a lot longer than technology. They're a lot less predictable too. People are interesting. And when technology helps people be more, well, people-y, it gets interesting too.

Remote work has always been a challenge—an understatement of the century—and that has only increased with time. One of the most limiting factors is that we always try to take a multidimensional world, where we interact with things based on their spatial presence and proximity to us and make it flat. Flat screens, flat people, flat presentations, flat content. Then we're surprised when these experiences fall flat. We scratch our heads and say: "Why isn't this remote experience as good as being in person?" We ignored the fact that most human communication is nonverbal. We wrinkle our eyebrows, we shake when we laugh, and we gesticulate wildly when we get excited, angry, or want to add emphasis. We smirk, we shrug, we hunch, we lean forward, we lean back, we cross our arms, we fidget. We are dynamic and restless and interactive and fascinating. But our enterprise collaboration technology did not allow for this. Life is not flat, but our technology was.

Several years ago, I became very interested in Augmented and Virtual Reality (AR/VR) and how AR—bringing virtual objects into my physical world—could improve remote work. So, for the past several years, my team has been building this. It graduated from its project origins and was released into the world as Webex Hologram: a multidimensional holographic collaboration system that delivers photorealistic quality holograms in real time. No avatars. No delays. No guessing games. Just bringing people together when they physically can't be, to share real and digital content the way they would naturally when face-to-face.

It's amazing technology, but I'm not here to write about the technology. I'm here to write about the story behind it. It's the intentional story of how I built a scrappy dream team inside of big tech, and it's the unintentional story of how I discovered my superpower—leading in ambiguity—by becoming an accidental intrapreneur. I learned so much about human dynamics, what motivates us, how to mold a team of unique strangers into a cohesive, self-motivated team of superheroes, how culture is crafted and cared for, and why it's important to have *Cake on Tuesday*. This book distills what I learned about leadership, innovation, and grit—and a few things about myself too. I hope you enjoy the journey and that it helps you on yours.

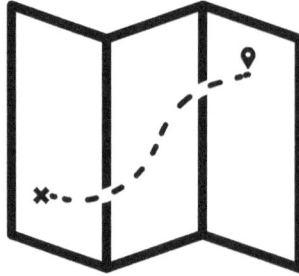

PART 1

Starting Is Hard

"The hardest part is starting. Once you get that out of the way, you'll find the rest of the journey much easier."

—SIMON SINEK

Because this is the story behind the story, I wanted to give credit to all the efforts that were part of the proverbial iceberg below the surface. We like to gloss over that iceberg, but starting is *hard*. I'm often asked to speak on innovation and emerging technology, but rarely do people ask: "How do you think about things?" "How do you come up with ideas?" "How do you persuade people to believe in those crazy ideas?" "How do you convince people to invest their blood, sweat, and tears into your vision?" Beginning truly is the hardest part, and that is why the lion's share of this book is focused on getting started.

Often, stories start with execution, or at least with building a dream team, but you shouldn't execute until your team is crystal clear on your vision, your process, and your culture and mobilized and empowered to go fast. And you can't build a team until you have crafted and sold a clear vision. And you can't craft a clear vision until you find your angel in the marble. And you can't find your angel unless you're looking for it. And before you know where to look, you need to ask a lot of questions. And before you can ask insightful questions, you need to be silent and think. And to be silent and think, you should probably go outside.

Starting is hard. But doing hard things is good for you. Or so my mom used to say.

1

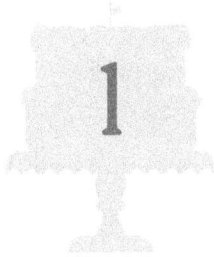

Be Disagreeable

"You cannot make an omelet
without breaking some balls."

—MARGARET THATCHER

"Good morning, I'd like to have an argument!"[2]

That memorable opener to a Monty Python skit has stuck in my head since my teen years. Sometimes, you need to spice things up and be a little disagreeable. I heard it said once that "if two people always agree, one of them is not necessary." To bring something new and different to the table, you have to be, well, different.

My Morning Argument

Webex Hologram never would have started if it weren't for an argument. Before I unwittingly embarked on this adventure, I was tasked with strategic alliances—working with some of our biggest partners in the industry on efforts that were impactful to the long-term strategy of both our companies. I was having coffee with my boss, who headed up both partnerships and strategy and not being one to keep my nose out of things outside of my domain, I decided to be jovially confrontational about the annual long-range strategic planning process that his other group was wrapping up and that I was only tangentially involved in. I recall saying something subtle and full of tact, such as: "Why do we call it a long-range strategic plan when it's neither long range nor strategic?"

I further lamented that, at that time, our process was to create a three-year incremental plan looking primarily at market adjacencies and only keeping a lazy eye on anything past that. But I argued that technology is always changing and can have a long tail. Strategy shouldn't be a three-year set plan; it should be a five-, ten-, fifteen-year, or more dynamic approach. And "strategic" isn't just looking at incremental changes to what's existing—it's seeking out disruptive change! What are the fringe, emerging technologies that can drastically disrupt our business?

The Way We've Always Done It

I may have been a little cocky in my armchair quarterback criticism, but one of my pet peeves is that sickeningly passive, innovation-killing statement: "This is the way we've always done it." I passionately hate this thought because it glorifies the status quo by implying that since something has worked historically, there's no need to change it because it will continue to work fine in perpetuity. What absurd logic! Nothing in life stands still; everything is dynamic. Accordingly, our processes, our products, and our approaches should be ever-evolving as well, and we should continuously strive for improvement. Without this constant sampling and revalidation, the default will be inaction, and over time, inaction becomes ineptitude.

Another reason I despise this statement is because it drips of false modesty by implying: *since* this is how it's *always* been done, who am I to think I can improve on it? It shirks responsibility by assuming that because the decision was made by someone else a long time ago, it does not require further thought. Abdication of thought is a dangerous and slippery slope. I think Grace Hopper summed this sentiment up masterfully when she said: "The most damaging phrase in the language is: 'It's always been done that way.'" Any time you encounter this sentiment in your line of work, pause, and consider if this is a good area to push back on. Sometimes the best things in life start with a healthy disagreement.

The Challenge

Bringing it back to that fateful morning argument, I can still remember the familiar hints of both amusement and frustration underneath the imperturbable expression of my *very* patient manager's face as he slowly sipped his coffee. As all of the functions I was poking holes at were under his domain, he was well positioned to counter my jab. In keeping with his always calm exterior, often belying the whirlwind of ideas, arguments, and counterpoints I'd learned over the years were always swirling through his mind at the ready, he simply met my gaze and flatly challenged: "You think you can do better? Show me." Game on.

2

Go Outside

You mean you never checked outside?

Several months later, when I pitched our executives on formation of a team to deliver this solution, it went something like this:

"Yes, you can have the people you are asking for."

"You can have a budget, buuuuut … there are some strings attached with that."

"Oh, and time.… That date you gave us for your first milestone, we're going to cut that timeline by 60 percent. You have four months to prove if something that's never been done before, and may not even technologically be possible, is real. Good luck!"

I could start there: in medias res. But so much of that story started well before that pitch, so let me take you back to the real beginning—the thinking and history that had been percolating for years that ultimately led up to that morning coffee argument.

Get Outside of Your Four Walls

I grew up in the geography and generation where the answer to any childhood complaint—"I'm bored," "I'm hungry," "I'm tired," or "I don't feel good"—was always the same: "Go outside!" I spent countless hours watching birds or bugs, poking things with sticks, and simply just going outside when something needed to change. That's likely so ingrained in me that it is still my natural reaction. Stuck on a problem? Go for a walk. Ideas all stale? Get some fresh air. Literally. Frustrated with a colleague? Walk it out while you talk it out. Humans were made to be outside. We crave sunlight, and there is something magically calming and invigorating about feeling the wind, hearing the birds chirp, and watching the clouds move through the sky. Whether it's an escape to a green space in the heart of an urban metropolis or a remote hike through the wilderness, there is something freeing about not having four walls closing in on us, even if just for a few fleeting moments.

Get Outside of What You Think You Know

Before we can even talk about innovation, we must talk about a prerequisite, and that is the simple willingness to admit you don't know everything. Much of corporate innovation is housed under corporate strategy. And we have this silly tendency to create a corporate strategy by taking smart people and doing something dumb with them. We close them all into a conference room until they crank out a palatable strategy that makes us *sound* smart. Instead, we should *be* smart and to be smart we need to admit there's a lot we don't know.

Talk to people in other businesses, other industries, other companies, other geographies, and other walks of life. Become well-rounded about your problem statement and what you're trying to find. Get outside of what you think you know. Ask an absurd amount of questions. The only stupid question is the unasked one. Ask them all. Then go outside your four walls. Literally. Go for a walk, breathe some fresh air, move your legs, exercise your lungs, get your heart pumping and your blood flowing, and gain a new perspective. Take time to think.

If you want to be a corporate innovator, I'll give you the advice my mother gave me nearly every day of my childhood: "Go outside!"

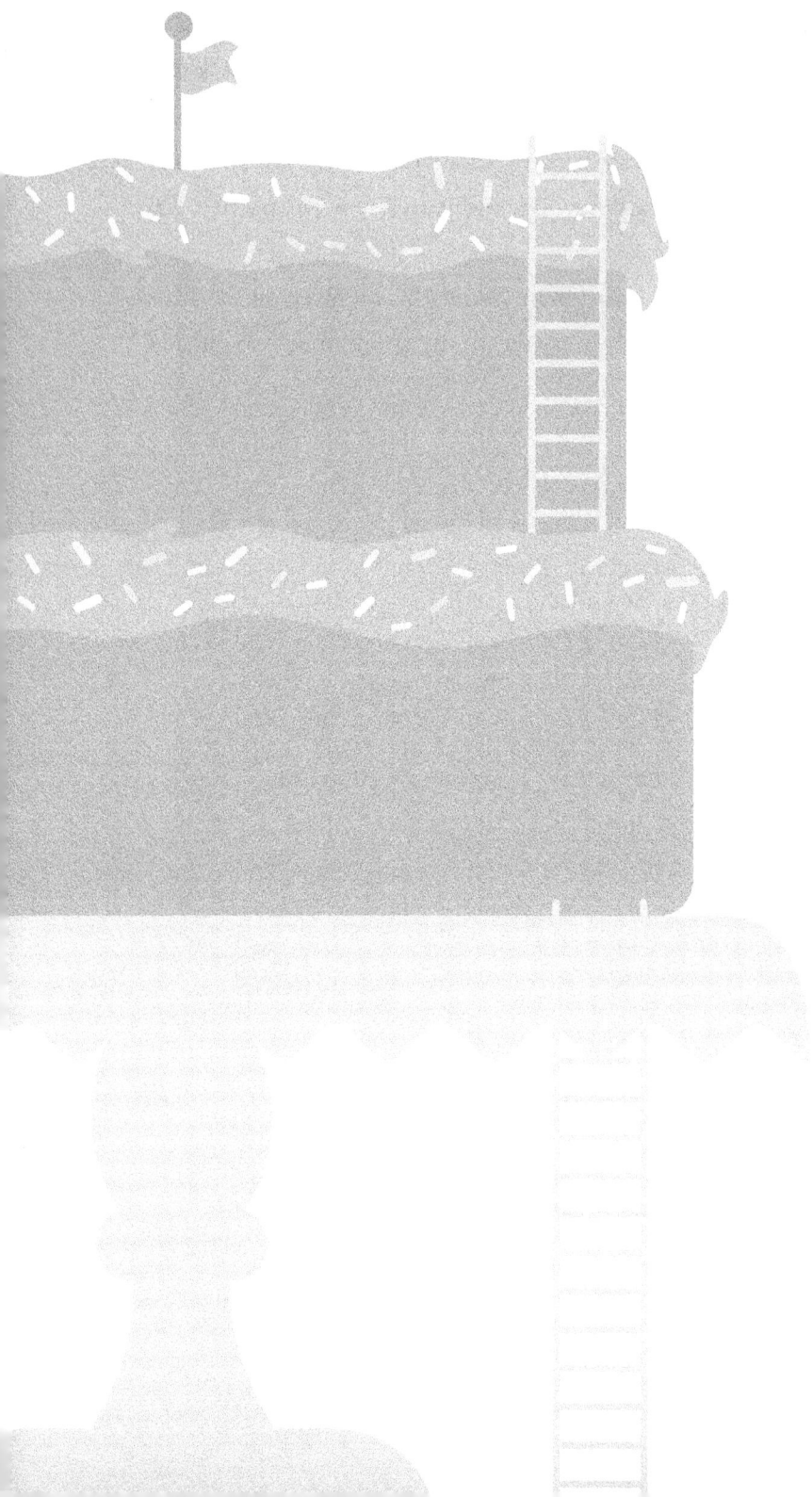

3

Find Your Angel in the Marble

"I saw the angel in the marble and
carved until I set him free."

—MICHELANGELO

If some part of your organization is not looking at completely off-the-wall, far-out potential, fringe technology, then your organization may not be around for the long haul. The reason you go outside is to expand your horizons and ask those big questions: *What assumptions am I making about our current industry, customer base, or product line that may be based on a shaky foundation? What has the potential to drastically impact our core business?*

The investigation phase of innovation is like playing Mine-sweeper. Each new area of knowledge unlocks a new connection you didn't know existed. Going outside means you actively embrace that you don't know what you don't know. The next challenge is to make sense of all those inputs and uncover a new, delicious insight that perhaps no one has discovered before because no one has had the exact same combination of unique experiences, conversations, learning, and events that your journey has brought about. This is where you ask yourself, "Why?" (my favorite question) about all that information you collected during your outside exploration.

Finding My Angel

Not one to say no to a long leash and a vague charter, I took the runway my then-boss gave me to think about long-range strategy, and I went outside the company and looked around. I went to every free conference, event, and expo show floor. I did every demo of every fringe technology from every two-person garage start-up I could find. I felt a bit like Will Ferrell in *Elf* taking all the flyers being handed out: "Thank you. Thank you. Thank you…." I went to so many developer conferences, standing out in my heeled boots and button-down amid the sea of sneakers and hoodies.

I was continually asked whether I was a developer or there to recruit developers. When I answered, "Neither," I'd always get the same confused smile and tilted head nod that implied I must be lost. I did get a lot of free T-shirts, sweatshirts, and backpacks, though. I talked to incubators, accelerators, angels, and VCs to see where they were investing. I listened and learned and experimented and I homed in on AR/VR as having the potential to completely disrupt enterprise collaboration as we knew it.

What resonated with me was how it could be used to change the way people interacted remotely. I wasn't interested in the technology itself; I was interested in the *experience* it could enable. I wanted to use holographic technology to teleport—to eliminate a screen as a divider reminding us that I'm here and you're there, but instead bringing me into your space or you into mine. I wanted to be somewhere I wasn't and have all the amazing richness of being together in person even though I was geographically separated. I wanted to see how we could use technology not only as a tool but as a bridge to bring us together. I could see my angel in the marble.

Be OK with Being Eccentric

It's OK to be the only one who sees it. It's OK to be a little crazy. (Personally, I prefer the term "eccentric.") People who changed the world rarely did so without someone (or everyone) thinking they were a few sandwiches short of a picnic. Even Aristotle, the father of formal logic, said: "There is no great genius without a touch of madness." So, don't worry; you're in good company. But your eccentric excitement must be genuine about something you truly believe in.

It's much easier to bring someone on a discovery journey to see your vision when you are genuinely excited about it. If you don't believe it, neither will they. A bit of a thick skin goes a long way here. This is where your grit will first be tested, because finding your idea is one thing, but giving your idea shape is a tricky and elusive business. Aaron Levie, CEO and founder of Box, aptly said: "Innovation is hard because solving problems people didn't know they had and building something no one needs look identical at first."

Once you have that idea, stick with it; foster it; protect it. If you believe in it, don't let it go. You've done the first part: you've found your angel. But seeing the form in the marble is only the beginning; now you must carve away the excess until the core of your idea emerges in perfect clarity. It's time to set your angel free.

4

Keep It Simple

To set your angel free, you need to remove anything not essential to the core of your idea. Your goal in removing everything else is to help your idea—just your idea—emerge in stark, breathtaking simplicity. I am obsessed with simplicity. Part of the reason this book is a short, snappy read is that I wanted it ruthlessly edited down to its roots. Considering Albert Einstein, a man known for his genius, had several things to say about simplicity, I figure I'm on the right track. As a nod to Albert, I'll break this chapter into three famous Einstein quotes.

"Everything Should Be Made as Simple as Possible, but Not Simpler."

Make sure the angel you set free is chiseled down to perfection and not a blobby nod to an entity with wings. Part of giving definition to an idea is deciding what to focus on and what to remove. In his enlightened book, *Essentialism: The Disciplined Pursuit of Less*, author

Greg McKeown says, "The reality is, saying yes to any opportunity by definition requires saying no to several others."[3]

Focusing just on what is essential and removing everything else require an incredible amount of discipline and ruthless diligence to avoid scope creep. My team is very familiar with me saying your minimum viable offer (MVO) should have a *big* M—the focus is on defining the minimum and continuing to keep carving down to uncover it. You are not trying to be all things to all people here (we'll get to that later when we shift to selling). Here is where you focus only on what's essential and remove the rest.

For Webex Hologram, we launched with just two use cases that were developed out of customer feedback: The first one was for remote training and the second for remote design reviews, especially for scenarios where sharing and teaching about a physical, not flat, object made it important to see both the object and the instructor simultaneously. We removed everything else.

There were scores of other great applications of the technology, many from customers directly. Because it was new technology in a new space, the possibilities were wide open. One of the engineers on the project recalled a simple MVO being highlighted on day one: "We all had a pretty clear view of what we were building and moving toward. I can remember hearing from the tech lead in the very first meeting an outline of exactly what the goal was to build—and so we weren't going off in a thousand different directions about what interesting 3D experience we *could* build—we knew what we were aiming for." We started every project phase with a crisp description of what was In Scope for that phase and what was Out of Scope. (Hint: your In Scope list should be able to be described in half a dozen bullets. If it can't, consider shifting some more things over to the Out-of-Scope list.)

"If You Can't Explain It Simply, You Don't Understand It Well Enough."

If your audience doesn't understand your pitch, they aren't going to buy it, fund it, or try it. Once you've defined your idea, you need to ensure you and everyone else on your team can explain it simply. If you or they can't, more work must be done. This is especially crucial in the fledgling idea stage when your "product" is just an idea you want approval or funding for. You may have been thinking about this for a long time and gone on a mental odyssey to arrive at your final conclusion that now seems glaringly obvious. But understand that when you go to pitch your idea, others have not had the luxury of that time or journey, so you will need to bring them on that journey of revelation extremely quickly. And to do this, you must keep it excruciatingly simple. If you are struggling with explaining it simply, take a page from Einstein and go back into learning mode to ensure you understand and are comfortable with all facets and counterarguments to your idea.

For Webex Hologram, we had multiple stages of pruning the story that resulted in several outputs, depending on time and audience. We had taglines for different purposes, the sixty-second elevator pitch, the short intro, the long intro; we recorded multiple videos introducing and demoing the experience and tailored for different use cases. We agonized over the wording of everything, and then every time we thought we got things just right, I'd try to say it out loud and find it was a tongue twister, and back to the drawing board we'd go.

After lots of trial and error, here are a few of the variations that got a lot of use:

- Short tagline: Photorealistic holographic meetings in real time.

- Long tagline: The industry's first real-time collaboration solution delivering photorealistic holograms.
- Short pitch: A holographic collaboration system that enables natural, multidimensional communication where people, objects, data, and ideas are not flat.
- Long pitch: Natural communication is spatial and multidimensional, not flat. Since the beginning of time, people have arranged themselves in circles to communicate, teach, and demonstrate. We rely on body language and gestures. We interact with objects and other people. As compelling as 2D experiences can be, they are always different from being there in person. They can never fully replace face-to-face. Because of that problem, we set out to invent a new way to travel. To replicate the feeling of being in a room together when distance makes that impossible. Introducing the industry's first, real-time collaboration solution delivering photorealistic holograms. It's an entirely new way of meeting.

In a later section, I'll talk about pitching to different audiences, but before you pitch to anybody, make sure you can say it out loud, smoothly, comfortably, and at a moment's notice. Make sure you understand it well enough that you can explain it. Anytime. Anywhere. To anyone.

"The Definition of Genius Is Taking the Complex and Making It Simple."

Lastly, don't mistake simple for easy. This is incredibly hard. Defining a simple idea, crafting a simple pitch, outlining an MVO. These are not quick and easy tasks. It's uncomfortable, painful, and laborious to chisel away the excess. It means you must sit with the idea beyond the initial excitement of it—the discipline and fortitude needed to do this keep many of us from getting from vague notions to exquisitely crafted visions. But that is what is required to put your idea into action.

I could say take the time to be slow and thorough here, and you'll be thankful later, but more plainly, if you don't take the time to be slow and thorough here, there won't be a later.

5

Always Have a Plan and Always Be Willing to Change It

"It is better to be prepared for an opportunity and not have one than to have an opportunity and not be prepared."

—WHITNEY M. YOUNG

There are two things I can say with certainty in all areas of my life: One, I've never regretted having a well-thought-out plan, and two, nothing in life has ever gone according to my plan. I do not see these statements as contradictory. Just like the adage that it is easier to steer a moving ship than to get one moving in the first place, it's much easier to revise and adapt a plan as new information and new circumstances arise than it is to hurtle along rudderless and hope you come out somewhere good.

Always Have a Plan

When I was brainstorming some ideas with a friend and former colleague many years ago, I recall him telling me: "The woman with the plan gets the funding," and I have found that to be true again and again. There are scores of people with good ideas but precious few with concrete plans to put those ideas into action. I credit my success not to my planning skills but to the practice of always having a plan and being ready to share it.

When looking back at the major decision points in the fledgling life of Webex Hologram, each of them was always proceeded by several months of painstaking plan-making:

- The decision to form a tiger team to explore the AR/VR space was made based on a proposal that was the culmination of ten months of prior research outlining industry changes, why we should care, why now, the risks of inaction, the potential market opportunity, and a five-step plan to unlock that potential opportunity.
- The decision to *go big* on AR/VR investment was made based on a proposal formulated over the previous three months of exploration by that tiger team.
- The decision to approve a full project team was based on a proposal that included a detailed project plan, including financial and people resources, technical problems to solve, and expected outcomes defined over the previous five months.

Fortune might favor the bold, but fortune also favors the well prepared. For instance, we knew that the life and death of Phase 2 of our project depended on a successful completion of Phase 1. Because of that, we planned out every detail of the experience. Like the often referenced, and famously linked with Maya Angelou, quote from Carl W. Buehner, "They may forget what you said—but they will never forget how you made them feel."

The whole idea of Webex Hologram was centered around a feeling: the feeling of being together with someone who was far away. Because of this focus on feeling, we wanted our executives experiencing the Phase 1 demo to feel something different from just an ordinary meeting or call. The way they felt mattered, and we were going for "Wow!"

You can't leave "wow" to chance, so every detail was planned. *What's the first impression you get when you walk into the demo space?* Our developers weren't thinking about that. I wasn't thinking about that. But our operations lead was and took the initiative to rearrange the waiting room, including pulling in office decor—chairs, a painting, and a plant—from across the campus to make the first impression more professional and feel like you were walking into an experience. Our demo was scripted. We spent hours talking through, writing down, and testing out:

- Who's standing where as each person walks into the room?
- Who's ushering them to a chair?
- Who's leading the demo experience, and what exactly are they saying, when, and in what order?
- Who's interjecting interesting factoids into the narrative?
- Who's intro-ing the waiting executives outside the demo room and briefing them on what they're about to experience?
- Who's debriefing the finishing executives on what they just experienced once they exit the demo room?
- Who's taking notes?
- Who's taking pictures?

And that was just the demo. Once the demo was done, our technical lead and I immediately sat our executive team down for a business discussion. The remainder of our demo team quietly exited the room. It was seamless and unnoticeable because we had rehearsed it several times before, and each person knew exactly what was expected of them and when. I then walked our executives through a pitch for Phase 2 of the project, defining the major milestones, necessary team changes, budget requirements, and a clear ask to approve and fund the path forward. We had a plan ready, and the woman with the plan got the funding.

Always Be Willing to Change Your Plan

It's crucial to have a plan, but it's equally important to be open to change. Be prepared to adapt and pivot when necessary. This is especially true in the realm of innovation since you are exploring uncharted territories.

You do not know what you do not know, so your adaptable plan needs to account for the continual incorporation of new information as the unknown becomes known. A former business contact comes to mind in this example. He was very good at taking in information and creating a preliminary operating plan of how to proceed. Still, whenever new information came in, rather than update his assumptions and adapt his plan, he would force the new information into his existing model and vehemently argue why his existing plan was still right. While his stakeholders valued his insights, he began to garner a reputation for being a "my way or the highway" guy since he wasn't able or willing to adapt to new data points on the fly.

Regardless of your brilliance, no one gets everything right on the first try. A little bit of humility goes a long way. You must admit that you don't know all the variables and your plan merely reflects the best path forward using all the information at your fingertips. The real value is in adaptability. As the adage confirms: the only constant is change. The best visual I can think of for this is watching a steady trickle of water navigate a downhill terrain. You know the water is going to make it to the bottom of the hill (clarity of goal), but as it encounters a clump of grass, a rock, or a pile of matted leaves, the water will twist and turn to adjust to this new obstacle, but always continue in a downward progression. Likewise, you should always have clarity of your goal, but the path to get to the bottom of the hill, or even where the ideal landing place will be, will change once your journey is underway. Remember that there is no such thing as a "final pitch" or "final plan"—there's just the latest version. Always keep it current.

PART 2

Set Your Idea in Motion

"Alone we can do so little;
together we can do so much."

—HELEN KELLER

Congratulations, you have started! You have given your idea shape. Now you need to breathe life into it. You need to build momentum, and that requires people. You need someone to fund your idea and champion it for you. You need people to build your idea, buy into your vision, and want to join you in bringing it to life. You need to lay the foundation to grow your idea.

If your idea were a seed starting to germinate into a wee seedling, you could think of this next section as everything you need to do to create the funds to buy the soil, fertilizer, watering can, and climbing trellis for your seedling to grow. This is where you find your building crew and draw up the plans for your greenhouse. You figure out what level of light and moisture and soil composition you need for optimal conditions. You have already envisioned the bountiful garden your seedling could grow into. Now, you need to lay the foundation to set the idea into motion. Get your gardening gloves out. We have work to do.

6

Nobody Cares Until
You Make Them

"I have become all things to all people so that
by all possible means I might save some."

—THE APOSTLE PAUL

Once you have the idea and define your clear and simple pitch, then you transition into a salesperson. You want to be an innovator? Congratulations, you're in sales now! Many people think coming up with an idea is the hard part. And it can be hard to distill the actionable nugget from the noisy clutter. But what's really hard is convincing other people to see your vision as clearly as you do. So much of *leading* innovation is actually *selling* innovation. And to sell effectively, you have to be all things to all people so you can meet them where they are and converse in the language and currency they understand.

Know Your Audience

Who are you trying to convince? Hint: it's not you.

To be an effective salesperson, you must be a chameleon, swiftly and smoothly adapting to each new environment. I always liked this definition of persuasion: "The art of navigating around someone else's mental roadblocks." In the early stages of Webex Hologram, we had a fantastic multifaceted designer who created several drawings illustrating our proposed system. Many of these had the content swapped out depending on who our audience was at the time.

Speaking to someone in healthcare or medical devices? Use an image of our solution featuring a heart and pacemaker model. Talking to an architect or workplace resources team? Use a virtual building as your subject matter. Pitching to a manufacturer or aviation industry executive? Use the illustration that featured the model of a helicopter engine being studied.

I can still remember countless customer meetings with our head of business development where one of us would be running through the intro pitch for the solution, and the other one would be waiting to see how the customer would respond and, based on that response, pull up one of a dozen decks with different sample imagery and use cases. This was a custom pitch on the fly. We were all things to all people so that by all possible means, we might convince some.

Minimize Pain Points to Make "Yes" Easy

Your goal here should be making it as easy as possible to get to "yes."

The first ask I made of our executive team in this space was a tiger team of five people to explore this area. I argued that our lack of knowledge about potential disruptions to our traditional business model put us at risk, so we needed to address this issue. I tried to think through all the questions and pushback I could receive and proactively address those in my presentation as well. I laid out a five-step proposal of how we could enter this space, with Step 1 being very close to something we were already doing.

Then, a second step, moving that thinking into a tangential area of exploration, then another step, and another, until the final step was my grand proposal for a future state. But my *ask* was to fund Step 1 with an out that you could reclaim that funding and those resources at any point. But, if we get to the end of Phase 1, here's what I think we can accomplish.

Make your ask bite-sized. Make it easy to get to yes. At this stage, the goal is to take the clear and simple message you have developed in the previous steps and tailor it to each individual or group you will be presenting it to. It is important to understand that there is no universal approach that will work for everyone. Therefore, it is necessary to put in the effort to customize your message for each audience, which can be a time-consuming process.

Beyond selling our executive team on why they should sponsor this effort, other groups also needed to be convinced. How do you get people at a big company to take a risk from their secure and known job to join an innovation project with a bold charter and unknown future? Again, the goal is to make the task as easy as possible: make it easy to get to yes.

From the individual's perspective, this was a risky move. This could be an opportunity to move them up the ladder, or there was the fear that if this didn't work out, this could cause them to fall off the ladder completely. So instead of moving all the people to report centrally into this new project, we left them in their host organizations and just allocated them to the project by phase. That way, there was an easy "out" at the end of each phase, and if the project failed, they still reported to their original host organization. It eliminated the biggest pain point.

When it came to selling to their management team, we took a similar approach by mitigating risk. Each phase of the project was defined in advance with a clear start, end, and exit criteria. There was no commitment from the person or their manager to go beyond the existing phase. We highlighted the amazing opportunity for them to be a part of something great if they freed up their resources and joined this phase of the project. We emphasized the value of being on the ground floor of the project and being able to say, "I didn't miss out on this. I saw the early signs."

A Note on Persuasion

Persuasion is an art form. The more you talk to people and understand their motivators, the better you get at selling. Don't be afraid to solicit help. There are many resources to aid in speaking, pitching, and crafting a pitch deck. Also, the more you pitch, the better you pitch. Practice, practice, practice. Run your pitch by anyone who will listen and record yourself making a pitch and make yourself watch it, critique yourself, take your advice, and learn from it. Rinse and repeat.

A Note on Timing

Timing is a major factor here. The market needs to be ready, and your investors need to be ready. You can't be too early or too late—every idea has a window of opportunity, and you need to be aware of where that window is and how long it's open. Once that window is open, part of being persuasive is defining the proverbial "burning platform" with a solid argument as to why *now* is the time for action and clearly pointing out the risk of inaction.

I'll close this topic on one final note of tough love: It doesn't matter how great a vision is; if you can't get anyone to see it, act on it, join it, or fund it, then it's useless. Harsh but true.

7

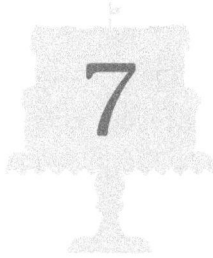

Rigorously Vet
Your People

"It's better to have a great team than a team of greats."

—SIMON SINEK

We've all heard the adage: "One bad apple can spoil the bunch," and I firmly believe this when it comes to building magical teams. While it is important to cherry-pick specific skill sets for the task at hand, attitude is everything. At the risk of adage overload, I'd also advise that, within a reasonable band of competence and aptitude, you should: "Hire for attitude, train for skill." Before joining our team, I would tell people in the interview process that we were a "no ego" team, and I meant it. We had PhDs and industry experts, but we vetoed some candidates because "I" was more important than "we" to them, which would not work with our defined culture.

Working lean means being willing to do whatever it takes to get the job done. I remember when our divisional head sat down beside our operations manager on the lab floor to help strip wires, the time when our senior software tech lead waited in line overnight at Best Buy to get a high-demand hardware part, and the day when our world-renowned video codecs expert spent hours unloading a U-Haul and setting up a lab full of equipment. None of them complained because they understood the importance of working together to achieve our goals.

Moving fast and working lean means you can't get hung up on titles and job descriptions. Everyone needs to pull their weight at all times (and sometimes more!). And they need to be comfortable building on each other's ideas in real time without concern about who had what idea and why we did or did not move forward with an approach. One team. One goal. We move and act as one.

On Hiring

Take extra caution when building your team (and identifying your advisors) because once you start running, you will need to rely on them to go fast, and you can't be second-guessing if they are backing up your culture. When making hiring decisions, have more than one person make this decision with you. In an ideal situation, it helps if you know someone who knows them or has worked with them, but that's not always possible. *Do* have someone on your interview panel who is good with ascertaining culture fit. It often helps if they are less embroiled in the technical expertise side of the business because being impressed with technical ability can overshadow truly seeing attitude.

When we originally formed the team that executed the first several phases of Webex Hologram, we were a small team that geographically spanned four countries and a nine-hour time zone spread. Many of us were meeting for the first time and had only four months to complete the impossible. We couldn't afford naysayers. We ran the effort with a simple C-suite style leadership team consisting of me as the "CEO," our technical lead as "CTO," and our head of everything else as "COO."

Any time we had to make changes to our team or add new people, all three of us had veto power on new hires. We each had a unique approach to how we qualified candidates, and while we may not have always understood each other's selection process or criteria, we valued each other's opinions. If any one of us felt a candidate could put the culture or performance of the team in jeopardy, we passed on that candidate.

As years and phases passed, our selection process evolved as well. I have found using a panel interview combined with a case study interview to be extremely successful in determining the fit of a new candidate. For example, when I needed to hire a senior business development manager, I put together a five-person panel consisting of senior and junior engineering, operations, and administration functions. I asked the candidates to pitch this panel on a proposed merger of any two companies.

The candidates were purposefully given no instruction or guidelines beyond that level of detail. The panel participants would listen to the pitch and then ask questions that arose from there. I would attend these interviews, but only to observe, and then solicit feedback from each of the panelists. I found the combination of seeing how candidates would handle themselves in ambiguous situations (delivering a proposal based on only one line of instruction) and interacting with a broad panel of interviewers from various fields and assorted levels of seniority gave me a very clear picture of how they would operate with this team under an innovation charter.

The ability to monitor but not interact in these sessions allowed me to be even more observant—taking note of body language and nonverbal communication. Then, receiving input from five other additional perspectives would either confirm these observations or challenge them to be revisited in subsequent interviews.

For more tips, tools, and templates
derived from hard-learned hiring lessons,
visit: **www.elizabethbieniek.com.**

Lastly, when hiring for an innovation team, home in on what jazzes people—what really motivates them and gets them excited. In the early stages of innovation, it helps to have people who, like Walt Disney, think "It's kind of fun to do the impossible."

A Note on Intrapreneurship

Intrapreneurship can have its unique pitfalls to navigate. When operating within the confines of a large company, it is important that everyone on the team *wants* to be on the project and isn't just assigned because of visibility or politics. When I pitched the formation of the tiger team to first explore and vet some technical viability in the AR/VR space, I was heading out the door on maternity leave with my second child.

Our executive team assigned a senior director, who was driving some other innovative efforts elsewhere in the organization, to lead the tiger team. The problem was, he was never asked if he *wanted* to lead this effort. He was interested in the project but had several other in-flight activities (and conflicting deadlines from some of his funding sponsors), so this tiger team became just one more thing on a long list of to-dos. I ended up taking the project back over after maternity leave because it hadn't gone anywhere, stuck on a backlog of rainy-day projects.

This experience taught me that the person leading your innovation effort needs to *want* to lead your innovation effort. It's not an easy road, so make sure they're motivated to take on the challenges that come with it.

8

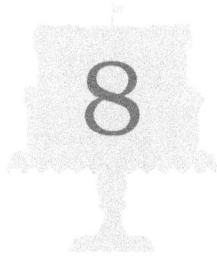

Make Room for Interpretation

"You can't always get what you want /
But if you try sometimes / Well, you just
might find / You get what you need."

—THE ROLLING STONES

Once you have your people, don't put them in a box.

I, of all people, should be open to this. I do not have the typical Silicon Valley pedigree nor a traditional career progression. The term "entrepreneur" was familiar to me even as a child. My family tree is peppered with interesting characters, both dreamers and doers. I have always been fascinated with the idea of ownership, and it's been a long-term desire of mine to start and run my own business.

I was not, however, familiar with the term "intrapreneur" nor would I have ever envisioned myself as an internal start-up founder running an engineering innovation product like a start-up inside of a large company. But life rarely follows the trajectory we think it will, or, as Bilbo admonished his nephew in *The Fellowship of the Ring*, "It's a dangerous business, Frodo, going out of your door. You step into the Road, and if you don't keep your feet, there is no knowing where you might be swept off to."[4]

I'm glad I was open to an opportunity that came in strange packaging.

Transferrable Talent

Along my nontraditional journey, I have had several excellent mentors and advisors who recognized the raw talent that came without a certificate, degree, or title and encouraged me to use and grow that talent anyway. I am grateful for the opportunities not to be limited by preconceived notions.

I've been so captivated by this idea that several years ago, I consulted with my husband as a silent partner in his firm, Baethos, a recruitment firm whose tagline was "empowering passionate people," which was built on this model of connecting people with attitude and aptitude to opportunities, regardless of their certification. It's built on the belief that abilities can transcend qualifications and skill sets can transfer across industries. Through my career, I have found those assertions to be true time and again.

Expect the Unexpected

Innovation is all about being open to the possibility of the unexpected. Apply that to your team as well. When you bring amazing people together and create an environment where they can take ownership and bring their best selves, don't be surprised when they do it. Expect the unexpected.

For Webex Hologram, our operations and logistics whiz also had a good eye for design and functionality. She had no formal training in this area but interest and aptitude. We ended up making part of her job be advising on the industrial design of our earliest prototype. And she crushed it. She also earned one of the first patents on the project through her innovations.[5] Her situation is also not the only one where I've had people who started on a team in one role for one project end up doing an entirely different role on the same or future projects.

Someone doesn't need to have a skill set listed on their résumé, or accolades for success in a field (or even to recognize their own ability), to be able to positively contribute in that area. Sometimes, people have interests or inclinations outside of their core expertise. Sometimes, people are just naturally gifted in an area or "have an eye" for something. Sometimes, people really want to learn or are fascinated by something that they accidentally become an expert in. Sometimes, you need a unique perspective or opinion. Don't shut these unexpected contributions down. Embrace them. At times, they will give your project the edge it needs.

At all times, it is important for your team members to feel like valued parts of a whole instead of being siloed into just one area. When people feel empowered and have ownership, their contributions can exceed your wildest expectations. So make room for their potential and allow them to thrive.

9

Define Your Process and Your Culture

Build a culture you want to work in.

When building your team, your process culture is crucial. This is where you go slow to go fast later. For my team, there was no room for egos and no "experts" versus "support" distinction. Also, despite being housed in our CTO office, I ran it like a start-up, not an engineering project. Beyond engineering, we also had product management, user experience, business development, operations, and communications. Various disciplines were represented, and every person had a seat at the table. One of our software engineers reminisced about his first impression of the project and said:

> I don't remember when the project started, but I do remember the first offsite: I mostly recall the collaboration precedent that we started at this meeting. The collaboration

of coming into a meeting for a new phase of the project with no one knowing how it was going to be done. We all felt like we were contributing in some way; directing the project in some little way. That was the glue of the team.

We made it clear that when it came to group brainstorming or discussions, everyone was an equal contributor and no one person's ideas held more weight than another's. Product management didn't build a plan without working in lockstep with business development and user experience. Operations didn't create workflows that would impact engineering without sitting down with them first and understanding needs and pain points. In *Multipliers: How the Best Leaders Make Everyone Smarter*, Liz Wiseman describes the benefits of a healthy, collective debate as a precursor to decision-making in terms of the "momentum it builds to execute the decision. As people debate an issue thoroughly, they develop a deep understanding of the underlying problems and opportunities and the imperatives for change. They put their fingerprint on the decision. Because they achieved a collective understanding, they are capable of executing collectively."[6]

When assembling our initial project team, we applied a "one for all and all for one" approach to planning and decision-making and this made us a stronger and more unified team as we all shared a common goal: to build the impossible.

Leadership Culture

This camaraderie extended beyond peers to our leadership style as well. Rather than a me versus them approach, I strove to let my team in on the action and let them know what we were facing and how we were approaching upcoming milestones. This was a delicate balancing act, as I'll talk later about protecting your team from unnecessary noise, but finding the right mix was crucial to allowing the team to be engaged without being bogged down.

That level of engagement may not be the same for everyone on the team, and that's OK. Some people are more apt to want to focus on their purview and not be overly distracted by things they can't influence, and others do best when they understand all the "whys" and how their piece fits into the whole. Working with your team to meet them where they are is part of the fun and challenging puzzle of leadership. You cannot lead a team of individuals collectively without getting to know and understand them individually.

Regardless of title, role, or responsibility, deep down, we are all the same. We are human, and humans are a complex jumble of hopes and fears and dreams and ambitions, likes and loves; there are things that motivate us and demotivate us, and real leadership is never a one-size-fits-all approach. To truly *lead* your team, you have to truly *know* your team. This takes time, asking many questions, doing even more listening, and a lot of observing. It means staying in tune with what works and what doesn't with each individual and trying to explain things in the currency they care about. It's treating them as the whole, complex, and unique human that they are.

While I did adjust styles with different individuals and dial-up or dial-down the level of detail shared based on their capacity or desire, I tried to be open about the major factors influencing the project. Letting them know what was at stake and why things were important allowed for more unified execution because we had a singleness of purpose.

Operational Culture

Your culture and operational process go hand in hand. Part of having clear roles is everyone knowing *who* is the decision-maker on *what*.

Each team member needs to be crystal clear on what decisions they can make on their own and what decisions require additional sign-off. And if they need sign-off, who do they go to, and what's the process? To create a framework for empowered decision-making, everyone should know where the buck stops, but it doesn't always mean the buck has to stop at the same place.

To revisit Wiseman in *Multipliers*: "When leaders play the role of decision maker, they not only carry the burden of making the right decision, they also are left to carry it through to completion.... But when a leader engages the team in making the most vital of decisions, they distribute this load."[7] To go fast, you can't have a single leader be the bottleneck for all decisions. You must define your operational culture, and this will allow more ownership across the organization and a clear distribution of responsibilities. This is not to be confused with process overload. On the contrary, a crystal-clear process helps you go faster.

Fun Builds Culture

Here's a process culture curveball for you: *Be silly*. If you're not laughing, you're not living.

Innovation icon Richard Branson admonished: "Fun is one of the most important—and underrated—ingredients in any successful venture. If you're not having fun, then it's probably time to call it quits and try something else." Once we got into a rhythm with Webex Hologram, we found that having short four- to six-month phases with a clear exit milestone worked best for the team. Each phase kicked off with an in-person three-day off site, and each offsite involved a carefully curated collection of icebreakers, problem-solving exercises, happy hours, walking tours, fun events, or some other "frivolous activity" that was part of the foundation for building a cohesive dream team.

That same software engineer recalled: "All of the special events that we did were a lot of fun.... We had fun together, which was another form of glue." Innovation is hard work, but working hard means it's that much more important to play hard. Don't mistake having fun as an unnecessary luxury.

10

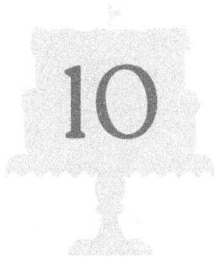

No Detail Is Too Mundane

"It's not a mundane detail, Michael!"

—PETER GIBBONS, *OFFICE SPACE*

The "measure twice, cut once" wisdom applies heartily to the planning phase. Nobody likes to talk about planning because it's not sexy or exciting. It takes a lot of time to do it right and can easily run longer than the actual execution phase. But this is quite possibly the most crucial phase of innovation.

One of our team members fondly recalled our approach of having short phases with clear planning at the start and clear exits at the end: "I loved it! At the end of each phase, asking if we were done, then celebrating our milestones, which I think was fun. It was refreshing and helped get ready for the next phase. In hindsight, we probably did not realize how healthy that was!"

When I received approval to form my launch team, we had a big, ambitious charter. We didn't know if holographic meetings in photorealistic quality could be done in real time. No one had done it before. Everything you saw out there was record and playback, or the quality wasn't great, or both. When I walked out of that approval meeting, I was only given four months to hit our first milestone—less than half the time I'd asked for. It was tempting to run fast. But you could accurately call this the "Don't start running until you know which direction you're going and who's carrying the water" phase.

Planning is about details, and no detail is too mundane. Just like in the first section of this book, when we talked about the importance of always having a fluid and up-to-date plan when gaining sponsorship for ideas, this importance continues in each ongoing phase of your project. Think of this as the drill-down plan for each area of your overarching plan, and now that you have a team, they need to be a part of the planning process too. Planning continues to be an absurdly crucial pre-step to every execution phase. If you mess this up, you don't have time to recover because innovation timelines are unforgiving.

Plan Each Experience

At our first in-person offsite, after the formation of the team tasked to build the first iteration of Webex Hologram, I prepared an excruciatingly detailed agenda. We had a lot to cover in three days, and many of the people coming had never met before. My operations lead and I crafted an agenda that planned down to the nitty-gritty details. We wanted to maximize the in-person time for effective brainstorming and team building, since my desired outcome of this offsite was a clear path forward and a gelled, unified team that felt like they knew each other. Not a small feat for three days.

We crafted a "things to think about before you come" list of sixteen unanswered questions to get people noodling on the same issues. Knowing the value of breaking bread to break down barriers, we started each morning with a hot breakfast in the room to be consumed during the morning kickoff. Knowing that many offsites lose participants at lunch, breaks, or transitions, we curated those as well, including onsite catered working lunches, and combining stretch and snack breaks to keep a draw in the room. Since many participants were from out of town and we were meeting in a high-traffic city, we arranged shuttles to take the team to/from dinners and a team-building event. This not only saved money by consolidating transport costs but also turned the transition times into great get-to-know-each-other events. Sitting in traffic on a bus for forty minutes next to someone you never met before but will be working with a whole lot over the next few months is a great way to learn about each other as a person. I overheard many conversations about kids, pets, and hobbies.

Culture doesn't happen by chance; it is crafted. And this crafting requires planning.

Planning Each Step

Just like I love a simple pitch and simple idea, I love a simple plan. I am also a big fan of phased planning and execution. That way, if outcomes are becoming too many or too complicated, you can break them into smaller components and move smaller pieces into the next clearly defined phase. Thinking in phases also eliminates the mental pressure to feel like you need to do everything simultaneously. Planning collectively with your team can be slow, painful, and laborious, but it creates buy-in and avoids the "I'm just doing what I was told" excuse. It is much easier as a team to hone in on your minimum viable output of a phase when you collectively define the deliverables to get there and know there will be subsequent phases to handle the other details.

A Note on Continuous Planning

This could also be called "empowered planning" because although planning doesn't end, you cannot always be there for every decision. You need to empower your team to plan on the fly. It's part of moving fast.

This is why we all have a seat at the table in the previous stage and collectively define deliverables. This is why defining your culture is crucial because it will be the framework through which your ongoing planning allows your team to stay on track while adapting to new inputs. To do this, you must let them in on the action and explain the "why." You must collectively plan clear execution phases: time-bound milestones, limited scope, limited and clear exit criteria.

If any phase becomes too complex, break it into smaller phases. Keep it simple. This planning approach is slower in the onset, but faster in the execution because it allows for ownership at every level. When you build this into your culture, you will find your team always striving for simplicity and clarity. Continuous planning becomes second nature, and it no longer feels like a separate planning function; it's just how you do business.

For more on crafting curated experiences and structuring your project with phased execution, download additional resources at **www.elizabethbieniek.com**.

PART 3

Add Oil and Reduce Friction

"There's always stuff to work on. You're never there."

—TIGER WOODS

"The road to success will always be under construction."

—LILY TOMLIN

The foundation has been laid! The proverbial greenhouse has been built. You've got funding and sponsorship for your project. You've assembled your dream team. You've set them up for success with a clear operational process and an instilled culture. The path forward has been made plain. Everyone knows their role, and things are in motion. Now what? Time to sit back, rest, and enjoy a well-deserved congratulatory cocktail on a job well done? Heavens, no, we've barely started!

Now that everything has been put into motion and is ramping up to full steam, this is the time to fine-tune everything. This is where you ruthlessly revisit all your assumptions and make sure what seemed rock solid in theory works in practice. If not, this is the time to change it. You should be figuratively walking through all aspects of your humming machine with an oil can and some sandpaper.

Where can you inject a little oil to make a good process become a great process? Where are things going slower than planned? Where are there bottlenecks? Where are things clunky? Get out that sandpaper and start sanding away at unnecessary steps or unhealthy precedents. Add oil. Reduce friction. Always be improving.

11

Don't Be a Flat Squirrel

"In any moment of decision, the best thing you can do is the right thing, the next best thing is the wrong thing, and the worst thing you can do is nothing."

—THEODORE ROOSEVELT

Being decisive was in the DNA of Webex Hologram from the start. The original executive sponsor for this project, Rowan Trollope (who wrote the foreword for this book), decided on the spot at the original "This is why we should care about AR/VR" pitch to fund my ask for a tiger team to investigate this space. He then decided at the following conservative/in-between/go-big scenario pitch that we would go big.

At the launch pitch of our project, he made an impromptu decision to fund our team and start-up costs on an accelerated timeline. Later, at our successful Phase 1 exit demo, he once again funded us immediately for our Phase 2 plan. Without being in an environment that valued decisiveness, we may not have had the opportunity to prove ourselves.

Momentum Matters

Although we faced some obstacles and challenges that required immediate decisions, we were able to maintain our momentum. The lesson to be learned is that once you have successfully directed your team toward the right path and have overcome the initial challenges, it is important to keep moving forward without stopping. My team is very familiar with hearing me say, "Action trumps everything." Being decisive is crucial for success, especially in innovative and uncertain situations. Making any decision is better than making none.

To apply this theory to your team in practice, make sure you don't have blatant or hidden blockers in your process that punish initiative. Any forward momentum is good, so when someone takes some initiative, takes a risk, or makes a tough call in your absence, celebrate, praise, and reward that—even if it's not the decision you would have made. It's more important that your team values decisiveness because as you grow, there will be more and more times when a decision is needed quickly, and you won't be able to be everywhere at once to make all the calls. Indecision can cause major delays, so it's important to encourage decisive thinking in your company culture.

When we were about four phases into Webex Hologram, I hired a product manager to replace some of my day-to-day activities. Things were getting busier, and we were trying to spin up another effort in parallel. I was also building an innovation model for repeat idea generation to build a pipeline of future innovation ideas. It was hard to bring in someone new in between me and the cutting edge. But to free up my bandwidth, I had to be willing to let someone else drive some of the planning, make some of the calls, and trust that he would carry on the culture.

We didn't execute things perfectly as everyone has their own way of doing things. However, we were in agreement regarding our mission and goal, as well as our team's operational model. After some negotiation and compromise, we began to work together seamlessly. This made me feel more confident in delegating some of the day-to-day decision-making tasks to others. As a leader, my job was now backing off the decisions that we had decided were now in his purview. They weren't always the same decisions I would have made, and I had to be OK with that. That wasn't the point. The point was that he felt empowered to own his role and I felt empowered to let those parts go and the team was clear on the transition.

In many cases, he was able to run at the same pace as the team, which allowed them to reach decision points even faster. Being faster was usually better. Above all, it was important to maintain our culture of decisive action. We brought in new people and empowered them to be decisive too. Eventually, he found a rhythm and worked together effectively with the execution team. This helped to replicate and expand our culture of decisiveness.

When It's Your Decision

Make decisions confidently. Your actions and values are observed, so avoid indecisiveness. Uncertainty, waffling, and delay are all progress killers. You can always course correct later if your forward momentum gets you slightly off target, but steering a moving ship is a lot easier than getting a stalled one started.

Live by the motto, "Action trumps everything." In their book of the same title, Charles F. Kiefer and Leonard A. Schlesinger (a former president at my MBA alma mater, Babson. Go Beavers!) put it this way: "Thinking and creating endless 'what if' scenarios doesn't help you. You can 'what if' yourself to death. The only way to know for sure is to act, reflect on what you have learned, and (to gain more learning) act some more."[8]

As a leader, you set the tone for your organization. They don't have a snowball's chance in hell of executing in a decisive culture if you do not lead the charge. Seeing someone else be decisive and get results, be decisive, fail, course correct, be decisive, and get results, does more than just model behavior; it lets you know what's acceptable and expected in that environment. This is an area where observation counts more than conversation.

I have been in other environments where the stated leadership mantra was that everyone is empowered to make a decision. But in reality, unless the decision made aligned with exactly what the boss would have done, it was bad news. Nothing kills a decisive culture faster than saying you want people to act and then punishing them when they do.

Don't Idle

Don't buy into the illusion that you have the luxury of time to make a decision. There is no such thing as inaction. Your lack of action simply takes you out of the driver's seat and makes you become the recipient of other people's actions. I am not advising you to rashly or blindly make decisions, but I do want you to be aware of the ticking clock, the proverbial burning platform. All opportunities have an expiration date, and the longer you waffle between actions, the more the landscape shifts around you, and you become the pawn, not the player. Don't get lazy. Don't buy into the myth that there is a neutral.

This topic always reminds me of a meme I saw once that said: "Be decisive. Right or wrong... Make a decision. The road of life is paved with flat squirrels who couldn't make a decision."

Don't be a flat squirrel.

12

Empowered Teams Power Through

"If you need any help, give me a
holler. I'll be upstairs, asleep."

—CLARK GRISWOLD SR.,
NATIONAL LAMPOON'S CHRISTMAS VACATION

During the team offsite for the third phase of Webex Hologram, there was a crucial partner event that conflicted. The project's technical lead and I needed to be at that partner event in Los Angeles, but my global team had all come together in person in San Jose. Both events had to move forward, and we couldn't be in two places at once.

This was still in the early stages of the project, and I had yet to hire our product manager to run day-to-day engineering. So, I kicked off the first day of the offsite, flew to LA with our technical lead, spent the second day at the partner event, and then flew back to San

Jose to close out the offsite. I had to trust that my team would carry on just fine in my absence. And they did because empowered teams power through.

Empower Your Team for Empowered Execution

The execution phase is where you get moving and go fast. This is where you rely on all the prep work in the previous planning and set-up phases so that everyone knows their role. Everyone knows the common goal. We've all collectively run through all the planning. Now we *move*.

For the offsite mentioned above, everyone knew their role. We had a clearly defined agenda and an outcome we were trying to achieve, and each person had a clear role to play in achieving that objective. The Cambridge Dictionary defines "empower" as "to give someone official authority or the freedom to do something."[9] If your team is empowered for execution, the absence of two-thirds of the leadership team shouldn't affect the task. They are a well-functioning machine and can continue independently.

Once you've clearly defined your objectives with your team, they should feel free on their own to be decisive and get things done that move toward that goal. This shouldn't just be a feeling, though; give them "official authority." State who has the autonomy to do what, and then reward initiative and decisiveness. This should be both clearly communicated in your operations plan as well as intuitive in how you operate on a day-to-day basis.

Remove Obstacles

Once you have established a team of superheroes who are experts in their respective areas, it is essential to avoid burdening them with unnecessary process and paperwork. Instead, try to centralize and streamline everything that can be taken off individual team members' plates. For my team, this meant our operations lead, Ashley, evolved to be our chief magic maker, who worked tirelessly and creatively to simplify activities like ordering, shipping, expensing, exceptions, equipment sourcing, vendor management, and approval tracking.

Ashley streamlined and consolidated all the processes involved, making it appear like magic to the rest of the team. For instance, if a piece of equipment fails and a replacement is needed, all you have to do is ping her, and the replacement will arrive on your doorstep the very next day. If you have something that's stuck in customs, just ping her, and she'll take care of it for you. And if you know what type of equipment you need but don't know where to get it from or how much it will cost, Ashley can help with that too.

You Do You, Boo

The reason you tirelessly remove obstacles from your team is so they can spend the maximum amount of time contributing in their lane. (This is also a big part of the secret for optimizing contribution and getting 10x performance out of a superstar team.) It is also incredibly refreshing, comforting, reassuring, and empowering when you tell your team members: "Just be you. We hired you because you're an expert in your field. Just do that. Be an expert in your field. Run as fast as you can in your lane. Don't worry about everything else. Tell me what you need to perform at your best, and I'll get out of your way and let you do it."

Note: this does not conflict with creating a "no egos" team where everyone is willing to pitch in regardless of title or job description. That quality is part of attitude: you want people who are always willing to do what it takes to help the team move forward. Removing obstacles, however, is about streamlining the process. While you want people who are willing to jump in and help wherever needed, you don't want them inefficiently bouncing from plugging one hole to the next. You should be creating a system where "hole plugging" is minimized. Removing obstacles is about creating an elegant, efficient system where each person is empowered to focus on their greatest contribution to the whole.

A Note on Leading in an Empowered Execution Phase

If you've set your team up right, they should be able to execute without you. Don't be scared by this. This is the natural evolution you're looking for. You want to remove yourself as a bottleneck. Your main job now is continuing to remove obstacles for them and being there just in case they forget they can handle this on their own.

13

Say It Once, Say It Twice, Say It Again So You've Said It Thrice

"The difference between the right word and almost the right word is really a large matter—it's the difference between lightning and a lightning bug."

—MARK TWAIN

Once you have defined your process and culture and have taken the time to build a solid plan forward, you have to communicate it. All of it. To everyone. Repeatedly. With documentation. And reminders. Again. Am I making my point that there is no such thing as overcommunication?

Make sure everyone is crystal clear on how things work, what they are empowered to do, and where they need to get approval. Communication is often touted as the number one cause of failed relationships, and business relationships can fall victim to this as much, if not more, than in any other relationship. Innovation, in particular, is a messy, noisy, and glorious business requiring even more precise communications around what, how, and, most importantly, why. Nancy Duarte is the long-standing CEO of Duarte, Inc., the largest design firm in Silicon Valley that is behind some of the most influential global business communications. In her *Harvard Business Review* article, "Good Leadership Is About Communicating 'Why,'" Duarte states: "In an ongoing crisis, clear communication is more important and more difficult than when things seem normal. Employees and customers are hungry for information, so we're tempted to pull together presentations and communicate with urgency instead of with careful planning. But if we present without addressing our audience's core questions of *what*, *how*, and *why*, we'll sow more confusion than we bring clarity."[10]

Running an innovation team is like leading through an ongoing crisis. Everything about the space, the industry, the technology, and the market opportunity you're tackling is fuzzy. That said, your communications shouldn't be. Just like climbers working together to climb an icy summit are connected by a rope with a series of anchors and the ability to self-arrest a falling comrade, so too communication is the lifeline that connects your team, anchors them to your road ahead, and allows them a path back to safety when they get too far.

Despite operating in a world of ambiguity, always communicate as clearly as possible with the information you have at that moment. When things change, as they regularly do in innovation, communicate again, as clearly as possible, in that new moment of time. Always be clear. Always be communicating. Always be *clearly* communicating.

Tailor Your Approach

Just as we discussed tailoring your pitch to your audience in an earlier section, that same amount of rigor is now needed to tailor your communication style to your team and stakeholders. Regarding staff and your working team, I've found it helpful for any important communications to:

1. Say it verbally in a team meeting.
2. Write it down in a team chat space.
3. Refer to the previous message or reinforce the message when connecting 1:1, because some people retain things better from seeing and some from hearing (and all from repetition).

When it comes to stakeholders, you may find someone asks for a weekly two-bullet update but then repeatedly comes to you with more ad hoc questions that could have been handled in a more extensive update. I find executives are usually forgiving of longer updates if they are clear, bulleted, and sectioned. For example, while a stakeholder might say they only have time for a one-liner every other week, in practice, it might work best to send them five short bullets on customer traction and five short bullets on engineering updates, with a single bullet call to action, clearly stating "None at this time" if no action is needed. And providing that little extra might save you a lot of needless back-and-forth.

I learned the hard way that the way people *say* they want to receive communication only sometimes aligns in practice with how they actually seem to retain communication. Observing what resonates and what doesn't might end up being more insightful here and allow you to create an effective style that is a hybrid of those two approaches.

Have Fun with It

For internal team communications, I started adding humorous gifs and emojis to all the "boring" types of announcements, such as things that were heavy in logistics or process. Gifs from *Star Wars*, *Star Trek*, *Schitt's Creek*, *The Simpsons*, and *Firefly* became regulars in my staff updates and corporate pass-downs. These became a bit of an art form after a while, and eventually, anyone on the leadership team who needed to convey a mundane message to the broader team turned to me to "spice it up." (Beware the reward for good work = more work!)

14

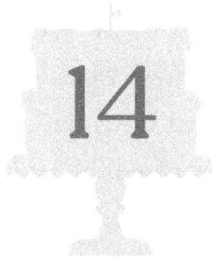

Have Cake
on Tuesday

Life is better when you're laughing.

Just because your head is down and you're crushing it doesn't mean you shouldn't be having fun. Quite the contrary. Some of the hardest times in my career were also the most fun. To ensure you and your team love the journey, take every opportunity to add levity to life.

Celebrate Everything

Celebrate everything: the good, the bad, the flops, the learnings, the inch of forward momentum, the birthdays, and sometimes just Tuesday, because why the hell not?

We celebrated everything that could be celebrated and tried to make boring things fun. In the previous section on communication, I mentioned that I started adding humorous gifs, quotes, and emojis to all mundane process updates or announcements. You might not be able to change a new tops-down tool requirement, but you can make an announcement about it that will have people laughing or at least smirking enough to take the sting out. Humor is essential to an enjoyable life, and even when we were deep in the trenches or things weren't going to plan, I liked to remind my team that if we weren't having fun, we were doing something wrong.

If you feel like you don't have a reason to celebrate, celebrate your people! Beyond just life events like birthdays or babies or buying a house (celebrate all those too!), celebrate people for being who they are. At the end of one phase, we did "superhero awards," and our ops lead and I spent hours coming up with corny real and fictitious superhero names and assigning one to each team member, cheering them on for one heroic attribute we recognized in them in this project phase. Some examples from this exercise that still give me a chuckle to read include:

- Our designer as Clark Kent/Superman: "Glasses-wearing UX designer by day, superhero by night that can step in and rig lights, calibrate a system, test a headset, report out on the latest industry news, or a million other things as needed."
- Our technical marketing engineer as Captain Elmer: "The glue that makes it all stick together."
- Our engineer applying machine learning to background removal as the Master of Disguise for his: "Ability to manipulate the background any way you want!"
- Our bald video codecs expert that joined after the first phase of the project as Lex Luthor: "If Lex used his powers for good… Because while you showed up late to the party, you came with your own resources and a reputation for ingenious engineering. Oh, and the matching hairdo."

We just meant it to be a silly little celebration tactic but found out later several of the team members ended up printing out and framing their "award" because it made them laugh and brightened their day.

If at any point you can't think of a reason to celebrate, there's nothing wrong with celebrating for celebration's sake. During a particularly drawn-out dry stretch of our project, there were no flashy demos or major milestones to celebrate. Feeling the need to brighten things up while we were heads down for months on end, our ops lead came up with the idea to do a *Wheel of Fortune* style "Wheel of Winning" that she made and spun at the end of each team meeting.

Whoever's name it landed on that week would receive a no-occasion rainbow cake in the mail within a few days simply because every day is a gift and even more so when you get to build something amazing. Our staff meetings were on Tuesdays, and remembering our weekly celebrations inspired this book's title: *Cake on Tuesday*. Also, who doesn't love cake? Mmm… cake…

Gamify Everything

It's unsurprising that celebrations and games became a core tenet of our culture because they were there from the beginning. When I first gathered this global team together for our very first in-person three-day offsite, it was a team full of various experts in their respective fields. Many had never met before.

Our charter was daunting. We had a giant whiteboard of ideas, and the clock was ticking. So, in the first hour of the first day of this action-packed three days, we strangers did the most important thing we could do. We broke into teams, assembled miniature drones, and raced them through an obstacle course in our conference room!

Drone racing at the start of our offsite immediately removed any expectations that this would be just like any other meeting or task force. It created camaraderie and unification toward a common goal. Nobody cared who you were: you could be a world-renowned expert in your field, but who cares? At that moment, could you get this two-inch drone through that twelve-inch hoop at the end of the table faster than the other team? That's all that mattered.

Forget about an icebreaker; this was an iceberg destroyer. Nine months and two project phases later, in a phase exit survey response to the question: "If you could have done one thing differently, what would it be?" one team member for whom this intro experience was still top of mind responded: "Learned to fly a drone before the first drone race!"

That gamification culture continued through the years. We did Lego competitions; a remote video offsite included breaks to compete on building and showing off the best at home charcuterie board. In one contest, we were doing a remote video offsite with our global team—each dialing in from their respective homes—and the challenge was who could build and throw a paper airplane the farthest.

Each contestant had to show their paper construction on the video call and then throw it and, on the honor system, measure the distance and report back. Our Ireland-based product manager won by throwing her creation out of her second-story office window in her home, because nobody said you couldn't do that! While we might have just set out to add levity, a constant culture of creative problem-solving that rewarded unique thinking bolstered Grace Hopper's belief that: "If it's a good idea, go ahead and do it. It's much easier to apologize than it is to get permission."

Any time things started to get a little tedious, we would find a way to gamify something and bring some fun back, because doing something hard needs an outlet for levity.

15

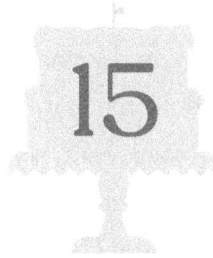

Get Out of the Way!

"If you continue to be a load-bearing beam
in your startup's tower, you'll never be able
to scale, grow and join the top of the skyline."

—RAND FISHKIN

This can be a hard one for modern-day leaders, but sometimes the best thing you can do is get out of the way and stay out.

Once your culture and process have been fine-tuned. Once the deliverables and timelines have been defined, and your team is empowered to do their jobs. Once your communications have been precise, clear, and received. Just stay out of their way. This means no meeting overkill, no unnecessary status reports, no hovering or micromanaging. Assuming they are continuing to meet deliverables, allow your team members the autonomy to execute as they see fit.

Don't Ruin the Cake

You've already done the work to streamline everything. When new obstacles arise, continue to adjust processes to keep operations as streamlined as possible. If you find something is not working, change it. If something is working, don't touch it. This is a little bit like baking a cake. (For some reason all roads lead back to cake!)

Once you've prepared the ingredients and sifted the dry, whisked the wet, and mixed them just enough but not too much, stop. Put it in the oven. Set the timer and walk away. If you start overmixing, your batter gets dense. If you start throwing in extra ingredients at the last minute, you compromise your creation. And if you keep opening the oven to see how it's going, you let the heat out and spoil the whole production.

If you've done the due diligence up to now to create this process, trust the process, trust the team, and let both run their course until the next agreed-upon checkpoint. And just like the cake, if something changes…. If smoke starts pouring from the oven or the power goes out, then you can jump in and help. But otherwise, get out of the way!

Leader → Coach

Your empowered team should also feel empowered to handle continuous replanning because planning doesn't end (especially in innovation where you're continuously traversing the unknown). Empowering your team to plan on the fly is part of moving fast because you cannot always be there for every decision, and no leader should be a bottleneck.

This is also why we all had a seat at the table in the previous stage and collectively defined deliverables. This is why we painstakingly planned clear execution phases with time-bound milestones, limited scope, and clear exit criteria. This is why we wanted everyone on our team to be able to recite their elevator pitch and our current phase's objective. This is why we wanted everyone on our team to understand what they were responsible for, the "why" behind it, and how their piece fit into the larger goal.

During the project's later phases, I stepped away entirely for the birth of my third child, and my product manager and operations lead stepped up to bridge the gap. They successfully and smoothly navigated the day-to-day operations while I was out. When I returned, because they were still executing with the same culture, rigor, and ethos, it was easy to slowly melt back in. I remember the first offsite after that maternity leave. The team was meeting in Dallas, and I was living in Austin. It was a short one-hour flight away, and I was still in the thick of full-on mom-ing it with my newborn.

I was able to come for the first-day kickoff, then fly back home that evening and nurse my baby that night and the next morning before flying back midday, spending the night in Dallas at a team-building event, closing out the next day with the offsite team, and then being home in time to tuck my older two into bed. Now, obviously, there were a lot of fortuitous circumstances there. The rotating location of our offsite happened to be nearest to my hometown, and I had the luxury of going back and forth. But I still recall the peace of mind I had at that time—and juggling the reinsertion into work after maternity leave while managing three kids between five months and five years at home is usually not associated with peace of mind. But I felt able to manage the juggle and slowly insert my way back into work because my beautiful, amazing, highly empowered team was doing just what they were designed to do—without me.

At this stage, you are switching from leader to coach, and rather than doing things for your team, you start reminding them or encouraging them to do things on their own. If things start getting too complex or with too many outcomes, break it into smaller phases (or better yet encourage them to define the subsets). Keep it simple. But always enforce ownership at every level. This avoids the "I'm just doing what I was told" conundrum. When you build this ownership and simplicity into your culture, your team always strives for simplicity and clarity.

PART 4

Leading through the Barren Middle

"I'm sorry to say so but, sadly, it's true that
Bang-up and Hang-ups can happen to you."

—DR. SEUSS, *OH, THE PLACES YOU'LL GO!*

You've been decisive. You've empowered your team to be decisive and take action. You've clearly communicated all aspects of your mission, culture, and operating model. You've imbibed your organization with fun and joy and celebrated all the milestones, big and small. You've created a culture you want to work in and your team can thrive in. And you've taken a step back to let your team shine and rise to the challenge, taking on more and more autonomy. And then...

No story is ever smooth. No seas are always smooth sailing. Sometimes, you hit the "Bang-ups and Hang-ups" along the way, and they threaten to throw you off course. Sometimes, you find yourself trudging through a boring, uninspiring, barren middle, and it's all you can do to motivate yourself to carry on, let alone rally your troops and lead the charge.

I wanted to write this next section as a nod to all the unseen hard work that happens in between the flashy beginning and the rewarding conclusion. The in-between is hard. Here are a few of the lessons learned that helped me stay the course. Godspeed, fellow traveler!

16

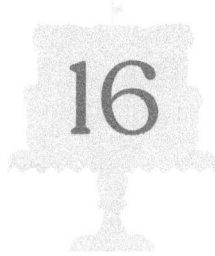

Never Stop Never Stopping

"Overnight success stories take a long time."

—STEVE JOBS

Andy Samberg's 2016 American mockumentary *Popstar: Never Stop Never Stopping*[11] seemed like the perfect title for this section on persistence.

Nobody Likes a Middle. Persist Anyway.

Persistence is a big part of this heads-down phase as you help lead your team through the barren middle. There's a reason why we call things a slog sometimes. There is a reason military personnel "embrace the suck." Starting is hard, but continuing on and on through the middle can be tedious—at times boring, and at other times downright infuriating.

As much as you try to operate as a well-oiled machine, as much as you do your darnedest to add levity and light to your days, unquestionably there will come a time when you: Just. Feel. Stuck. There will be times when you feel like you're wading through molasses on a cold day. Maybe outside forces are actively derailing you. Maybe it's a mental struggle to keep the end in sight.

If this is where you're at, persist, even when you don't feel like it. Persist. Even when it's painful. Persist. Even when you feel like literally banging your head against a wall would be more productive. Persist. Nobody likes a middle. It's not momentous. It doesn't have the excitement of a beginning or the satisfaction of an ending. It's just more of the same: putting one foot in front of the other. And sometimes the slog is just that: a *slog*. This is where most people give up. Don't. Persist.

Don't Stop at Three

Probably one of the best pieces of advice I've ever received on pushing through came from outside the office. Several years ago, in the BK phase (before kids) of my life, when I had an excess of this thing called time, I decided I wanted to run the San Francisco Half-Marathon. It's a beautiful 13.1 miles from the baseball stadium along the Embarcadero to the Golden Gate Bridge and back.

The only problem was, I hadn't run any distance more than a couple miles since I was a teenager, and nothing longer than five miles in my entire life. I followed a couch potato to 5K plan to get me slowly started and ramped up to be able to repeatedly run three miles without feeling like I was going to die. And then I got stuck. Any time I tried to run more than three miles I would become completely exhausted in that last half mile and just end up having to stop at three. I thought that might be my limit.

So I started researching how to get past a plateau when you're stuck and I found this great article that promised the secret of going from a three-mile run to a five-mile run. It explained that if you could already run three miles, you were physically capable of running five miles. It wasn't a physical limitation you were encountering. It was a mental one. The trick to running five miles was this. Are you ready? "Don't stop at three." Period. Simple. Done. That was it.

Despite feeling a bit jaded by this absurdly simple revelation, I realized its hard truth and simple wisdom. Sometimes, there is no trick, no secret. It's just simple, stubborn persistence. Sometimes that's all you need. Sometimes you have to remind yourself to keep going and don't stop at three. (By the way, in case you were wondering, I did complete the San Francisco Half-Marathon that year. I even have the bobblehead to prove it.)

This Too Shall Pass

One of my most painful "middle moments" was a particularly excruciating five months between receiving approval for funding and actually receiving the said funding. In many cases, building an internal start-up inside of a large company is the best of both worlds: speed and agility of a start-up plus security and resources of an established entity. Sometimes, however, this nontraditional model can experience the worst of both, and we once got caught up in a perfect storm of annual planning, fiscal year-end deadlines, management changes, and conflicting priorities such that we were in full holding pattern for five months just waiting to be able to move money from the left hand to the right.

It was beyond painful. It had the potential to be incredibly stressful, until I had to just let go. After I did all the communications, and recommunications, and appeals, and escalations, and once I had exhausted all the active measures available to me, I simply had to wait. And in the words of Inigo Montoya, "I hate waiting."[12] But there is no use in agonizing over circumstances outside of our control. Sometimes we just have to tighten our belts, put our heads down, and embrace the suck. This too shall pass.

When the Going Gets Rough, Lean into Your Culture

If you think of the previous two sections of this book as all about creating the plan, team, process, and culture to move your idea from concept to execution, this is where you rely on that plan, team, process, and culture to carry you through. As Bill Withers said in his iconic song: "Lean on me / When you're not strong / And I'll be your friend / I'll help you carry on / For it won't be long / Till I'm gonna need somebody to lean on."

Lean into the strong foundation you have created. It will carry you through this barren middle until you exit the other side. One foot in front of the other. Don't stop now. Never stop never stopping.

17

Be an Umbrella and a Shield

"I attribute my success to this: I never gave or took an excuse."

—FLORENCE NIGHTINGALE

"Remember, there are no bad crews, only bad leaders."

—MASTER CHIEF JOHN JAMES URGAYLE, *G.I. JANE*

While you might be staying out of the way, allowing your team to execute like the finely oiled machine you have empowered them to be, you are not idle. You are actively working to protect your people. Your people are the heart and soul of everything you do. Your dream would not have come to life if your people hadn't invested their all to bring it to life. So protect them.

Protect in All Directions

I like to think of myself as an umbrella and a shield for my team—nothing gets to them without first having to get through me. As an umbrella, you are responsible for keeping the rain off their heads. The expression that "sh*t rolls downhill" should not bother your team, because you are a protective barrier for them.

Protect them from the noise. Protect them from the barrage of unnecessary distractions that you, as a leader, may need to tussle with regularly. Your team doesn't need that distraction; that stops with you. As a shield, you protect them from the constant arrows of doubt, criticism, and all the crappy red tape being fired at them in an attempt to knock them off course. This is also why you streamlined everything for them.

Keep the Sharks to Yourself

I once saw a painting of a father carrying a child through the water. The viewer's vantage point was that you could see both above the water—the child dry, safely in her father's arms, the warm sun shining, and a smile of laughter on her face—as well as below the water—the sharp rocks, coral, and circling sharks the father's feet were navigating below the surface.

This imagery reminds me of leadership. I'm not implying that your team members are your children, but as a mother of three, I can't help feeling fiercely protective of my team. There are things they don't need to know. There are burdens they shouldn't have to carry. And there are fears they don't need to face. In leading through a multiphase, multiyear project, there were many times when I risked sponsorship changes, funding decreases, and even cancellation of the project entirely.

Until there was a specific action my team could take in the face of a challenge, in most cases, I never told them what we were up against. If there was nothing they could do, there was no point in causing them stress for something that might never happen. That was *my* job, to find a way through for the team so they could keep going forward. I felt validated in a comment from an anonymous survey of the team after the second phase of our project. In addition to soliciting feedback on what I could do better as a leader, our ops manager had also asked the team: What was your favorite thing Elizabeth contributed to the team? One team member responded: "I know that I don't have any idea of the extent of her contribution. Maybe that is my favorite." Sometimes, I needed their help, and I looped them into what we needed to do and why. Many times, they never knew.

Protect your team from unnecessary noise.

Have Your Team's Back

In protecting your team from outside forces, make sure you also protect them from you. I am a firm believer in two leadership adages:

- *"If the team succeeds, it's because of them. If the team fails, it's because of me."*

  Period. No exceptions. Sadly, this is a more and more rare quality of leadership, but in my opinion, this is Leadership 101. You shouldn't be a leader if you're not ready to accept this as a nonnegotiable truth.

- *"Praise publicly, punish privately."*

  And not only praise publicly but praise often. Build your team up. Reward small efforts in the right direction. Punish privately, but don't avoid it when necessary—part of protecting is correcting—you are making your team better and stronger.

My right-hand person through thick and thin for nearly a decade is Ashley. I mentioned her earlier in this book as our chief magic maker, COO, and operations lead turned industrial designer. She once told me something that has filled me with immense pride:

> I absolutely love how you have my back and I never ever ever feel like I am alone in something or out on the limb, bobbing in the breeze just hoping not to fall when big, bad, [corporate] blows their wind at me. You show up every single time I need you and you step in front of me to fight the battle and protect me from the bureaucracy that they try to impose so we can hardly do our jobs. You are a safe place for me, my words, my feelings and what I am trying to do/ accomplish. You also give me a place to grow, build, and shine, and you encourage me to do it. Once I think you think I can do it, I think: if SHE thinks I can do it, I must be able to! Then I go and get 'er done.

This is what I aim to do, and if I did nothing else right, I was enough of an umbrella and a shield for one person that allowed them to feel the confidence that they could do and be more. Quite frankly, there is nothing more important.

18

Don't Get Lazy

"I got him. I got him!"

—LUKE SKYWALKER

"Great, kid. Don't get cocky."

—HAN SOLO, *STAR WARS: EPISODE IV—A NEW HOPE*

You did it! You formed and fashioned a team and led them through shark-infested waters to an amazing outcome. You did it! You've arrived! You're done!

Wrong!

Don't coast. Don't slack. Don't get lazy. There is no "done." Don't get cocky.

Know Why It Worked

You did it once, can you do it again? Why was it successful? Can you translate your experience into a repeatable model of success? Could you teach someone else to do it? Think through what worked, what didn't, what could be improved, what you learned.

Can you create a system out of it? Constantly ask your team: *How can we make things better?* Postmortem reviews are a great way to solicit feedback from all parties involved. Anytime you wrap up a project, phase, or milestone, solicit an active review from your team on how to improve. We were in the habit of asking for honest feedback at the end of each phase. Below is a subset of the questions our ops manager posed to the team members after our first two phases:

- What would you change about [ABC Person's role as XYZ Lead], or how should it operate differently going forward?
- How did the task tracking system work for you and how can we improve it?
- If you could do one thing different, what would it be?
- How effective were the reoccurring workstream sync-up meetings? What would you change?
- What was your favorite thing XYZ Lead contributed to the team?
- Do you feel being part of this team helped grow your career?
- Where did we get lucky?
- How effective were the offsites and what would you change (location, structure, activities)?
- What did you like least about being part of this team?
- Did you feel being part of this team helped you grow as a person? If so, how?
- Other feedback?

These questions are by no means perfect. They evolved each phase, and over time as additional trust was built in the team, we were able to replace blanket survey questions with in-person and virtual coffee sessions to have a frank, honest dialogue about what worked, what didn't, and how we could improve.

Soliciting feedback also isn't something that should be reserved just for postmortems either; having a culture of continuous improvement will make it easier for you to solicit regularly and for your team to regularly provide feedback. It also takes the stigma out of it when it's reframed away from "Tell me what I did wrong" to "How can we together make this better?"

Always be listening. Always be asking. Always be improving.

Protect Your Creation

Just after victory is when you are most vulnerable. That's when people start slacking off or relying on momentum or inertia. And that's when things get sloppy, and the wheels start falling off. Once you have done all that work to create a dream team and a magical culture, *protect it*. It sounds obvious, but it's not. It sounds easy, but it's not. This is hard because it's not on fire.

Expel the Myth of Neutral

I've heard life described as a conveyor belt. You are either actively moving toward your goal or life is slowly pulling you away. There is no such thing as standing still. Order is not the natural state. Entropy is. Trust me, I have three small kids. My house is the perfect example of this.

Entropy is the natural state. If you stand still on a treadmill, you go backward. So don't get lazy. Just as with exercise, you don't achieve a level of physical fitness and then just stop and expect to stay at peak performance. It requires constant maintenance. It's the same with leadership, driving a team, and creating a culture. Don't coast. Don't get lazy. We think after we do all that work to set it up, it just goes on, in perpetuity on its own. It doesn't.

Protect Your Culture

Culture is fluid and fragile. Once you've created it, foster it and fight to protect it. You've built a team that has the most valuable quality—trust. Once y'all have earned that, ferociously protect that trust. Sometimes, you need to get a little touchy-feely about it. I closed every three-day offsite with an exercise to go around the room and say one thing about the person next to you—one thing you learned by conversation about them over the last three days, and one thing you learned by observation.

It had to be something surprising, interesting, or uplifting. How often has one of your direct peers—someone you admire and respect and an expert in their field—told you something you did that impressed them? How did that make you feel?

Creating dynamic teams doesn't happen by accident. Culture is crafted.

19

Be Careful Who You Listen To

"Death and life are in the power of the tongue, And
those who love it and indulge it will eat its fruit
and bear the consequences of their words."

—PROVERBS 18:21 AMP

In the last section of this book, I'll talk a little about the kick-in-the-pants motivation that can sometimes come from hearing "no." However, especially when you persist through the barren middle, be very careful who you are listening to. Having good mentors in your corner that you can use as a sounding board, and who will tell you the cold, hard truth when you need to hear it, is essential.

"Without counsel, plans go awry, But in the multitude of counselors they are established" (Proverbs 15:22 NKJV). This is life-giving. This is a refreshing drink on a parched throat. Find these people. And once you've found them, value them. But the other side of that coin exists as well. Doing the impossible attracts the naysayers. Watch out for them. Stay attuned to the underlying motivations of the speaker to know who they are.

Build a Mentor Cabinet

Mentorship does not have to be a formal relationship. In fact, most are not structured mentor/mentee arrangements. By mentor, I mean someone who has gone where you're trying to go and learned a thing or two along the way. I think people often get caught up in thinking they need to find someone exactly like them, traveling their exact journey, just several leagues ahead. You don't need to be that specific.

I have different mentors for different areas of my life, and I go to them for different reasons. A spiritual mentor can be a fantastic accountability partner to help me prioritize my focus areas and strengthen my spiritual journey. But I wouldn't ask them for specific business advice or to build my fitness regime. I might have someone who is a guru at politically savvy communications, and when I need to navigate a particularly thorny negotiation, they might be the person I ask to spend five minutes eyeballing a communication and letting me know their gut reactions. They don't need to know the specifics of my business, industry, or even people involved.

Every pitch deck I have ever created has been tried out at least once, and usually many times, to many different people before it is ever pitched to its final intended audience. Every time you make a pitch, or walk someone through an idea, not only do you get a better understanding of it yourself, but you will get feedback—both verbal and nonverbal—about how to make it better.

Every time I have navigated a career move or made any major decision, I have asked for advice. Advice is free. Take all you can get. And the more you have, the more likely you will see patterns emerge, and you will be able to pull out the nuggets of truth to help you move forward. Solomon, considered the wisest man on earth, said, "In the multitude of counselors, there is safety" (Proverbs 11:14b NKJV). Having a cabinet of good mentors to pull from will help you course correct as needed and safeguard yourself and your ideas.

Watch Out for Crabs

That being said, beware of the crab mentality. This is derived from descriptions of how crabs in a crate behave. Anytime one is starting to climb out, the others will grab it and pull it back down. Whether intentional or unintentional, be wary of any humans that act like crabs. Intentionally, this could be part of the "if I can't have it, neither can you" mindset that is spurred on by envy, jealousy, or resentment.

In many cases, though, it is not overt and intentional sabotage that does the damage, but rather unintentional negative or dismissive comments that can be dream killers even if they aren't meant as such. Oftentimes these could even have nothing to do with you or your project, but merely be a person speaking from frustration with their own current situation and a host of other unseen factors.

As Dostoevsky put it in *The Idiot*, "Don't let us forget that the causes of human actions are usually immeasurably more complex and varied than our subsequent explanations of them." Be aware that anyone can have a bad day and make a negative comment they didn't fully intend, but be *very* wary of the Negative Nancys and Doomsday Donalds in life. Protect your ideas (and yourself!) from them. Negative energy can pollute your inspiration well before you realize the poison has even started leaking in.

Prune Your Loops

Criticism is a tricky area. You want constructive criticism to help you improve your ideas, your pitch, and your approach. And you want harsh criticism to help you steel your resolve and toughen you up because you will encounter it in your journey, and it's good to have a few test battles under your belt before you face your first Dream Crusher opponent.

But be careful of the extremes. The overly positive feedback: "I think all your ideas are so good!" The people who think every idea you have is genius. It may feel fantastic for your ego, but it will give you a false sense of confidence and is not valuable criticism. You need true feedback. On the flip side, some people like to poke holes in things. Be wary of the time wasters as well. If their criticisms are helpful and spur you on to create a better idea, then by all means, keep going back for more. But if they like to hear themselves talk and bring up all the rare <0.1 percent scenarios where things could go wrong, just cut them loose.

Ruthlessly and regularly prune your feedback loops. Understand why you have feedback. Feedback is to make you, your process, or your product better. Period. That simple. Neither the "This is great, it's really fantastic!" nor the "This is dumb, it'll never work" are useful for that purpose, so cut them out.

20

Sometimes You Have to Be Your Own Cheerleader

"To bear a ring of power is to be alone."

—GALADRIEL, *THE FELLOWSHIP OF THE RING*

(2001 SCREEN ADAPTATION)

If you want to lead in innovation but you don't have a thick skin, grow one really fast. You're going to have to get used to hearing: No; That's not possible; It's not going to work; We've never done that before… and a slew of other not helpful noise.

Listen to Your Gut

In all your feedback gathering, don't forget checking in with yourself. While there is wisdom in many counselors, it's also important to realize no one can lead you where they've never been. Sometimes you must blaze your own trail. Listen to yourself. Don't discount your gut feeling. Malcolm Gladwell's book *Blink* is a fantastic read on the science behind gut feelings and why you should listen to them.

If everyone is telling you to go right and you, down to your core, feel that is wrong, you should go left. Check your fears. Check your ego. Check your assumptions. But if they all check out, go with your gut.

Keep Some Encouragement on the Ready

When you're building or birthing something new, you might have to go it alone, but that doesn't mean you don't still need encouragement and the occasional pep talk. How do you make sure you don't get depressed, dejected, or dissuaded by roadblocks? While it helps to be naturally optimistic, sometimes injecting a little optimism into the situation from a tried-and-true source is a good safety net. For as long as I can remember, I've kept a quote book of inspirational quotes for those times when I need to be my own cheerleader. These are a few of my favorites:

On Embracing the Suck

- "You do not achieve anything without trouble, ever."—Margaret Thatcher
- "Life is not easy for any of us. But what of that? We must have perseverance and, above all, confidence in ourselves. We must believe we are gifted for something and that this thing must be attained."—Marie Curie
- "The world is not the most pleasant place. Eventually, your parents leave you and nobody is going to go out of their way

to protect you unconditionally. You need to learn to stand up for yourself and what you believe and sometimes, pardon my language, kick some ass."—Unknown, often incorrectly attributed to Queen Elizabeth II

- "Women are like teabags. We don't know our true strength until we are in hot water."—Eleanor Roosevelt

On Persistence

- "A hero is no braver than an ordinary man, but he is brave five minutes longer."—often attributed to Ralph Waldo Emerson
- "I firmly believe that any man's finest hour, the greatest fulfillment of all that he holds dear, is that moment when he has worked his heart out in a good cause and lies exhausted on the field of battle—victorious."—Vince Lombardi

On Leveling Up Your Thinking

- "A ship in port is safe, but that's not what ships are built for." —Grace Hopper
- "Therefore we do not lose heart. Though outwardly we are wasting away, yet inwardly we are being renewed day by day. For our light and momentary troubles are achieving for us an eternal glory that far outweighs them all. So we fix our eyes not on what is seen, but on what is unseen, since what is seen is temporary, but what is unseen is eternal."—2 Corinthians 4:16–18 NIV

- "I went to the woods because I wished to live deliberately, to front only the essential facts of life, and see if I could not learn what it had to teach, and not, when I came to die, discover that I had not lived."—Henry David Thoreau

When things are not going as well as you'd like, there's no value in throwing yourself a pity party. Get up. Dust yourself off. Put one foot in front of the other. And carry on. There is always a light at the end of every tunnel. If you don't see it yet, keep walking. And if your quote book pep talk doesn't do the trick for you, I'm pretty sure my mom's wisdom from chapter 2 also applies here—"Go outside!"—and let nature cheer you up.

PART 5

Insights from the Rearview Mirror

"Wisdom cannot be rushed. It comes in its own time."

—UNKNOWN

Many of the lessons learned so far were ones I learned through trial and error, common sense, wisdom of the ages or divine inspiration, or entirely on accident through plain dumb luck. There are some revelations, however, that only come later, when looking at the journey from the rearview mirror. In this closing section, I attempt to capture some of those lessons I either had to learn over and over again before they stuck, or I didn't realize them until looking back on how far we'd come.

21

Sometimes the Best Thing You Can Hear Is "No"

"The brick walls are there for a reason. The brick walls are not there to keep us out. The brick walls are there to give us a chance to show how badly we want something. Because the brick walls are there to stop the people who don't want it badly enough. They're there to stop the other people."

—RANDY PAUSCH

This was a hard lesson to swallow. Hearing "no" is not pleasant. It doesn't feel good. It stirs something up in you. A little bit of soul-crushing defeat, but just a little bit more of a defiant: "Oh yeah? Hold my beer. Watch this!" spirit. The lesson I had to learn the hard way was that hearing "no" was sometimes the only way I would ever get to "yes."

Oh, Yeah?

I should have clued into this during my undergraduate education. There was a program at my school that if you could find a professor to sponsor your work, and you received majority approval from the heads of your department, you could create your own three-credit independent study course.

I found my sponsor, wrote my draft proposal, and presented my concept to the committee for review in advance of submitting the final proposal. The chair of the department told me my idea was no good and I would "never get this approved." That was many, many years ago and I still remember exactly how I felt: a young, unsure of myself kid, tentatively proposing an idea to a celebrated expert twice my age, and being told boldly, with utter confidence, that I would "never" succeed in this venture. It was intimidating. I felt deflated, scared, even more unsure of myself. And even still, a little voice in my head was screaming: "Oh yeah? Watch me prove you wrong!"

In that case, I don't know if he was trying to inspire and push me to greater heights. I don't know if the revisions and work I put into the final proposal swayed his opinion or if he thought the whole idea was garbage and continued to vote it down in the final review. I'll never know. I don't need to know.

All I know is my final proposal was approved. And the lesson stuck with me: even if someone with more experience, more years, more tenure, more position, more power, more authority, more confidence, more anything … tells you you can't, that's just one opinion. It doesn't define your future. Sometimes, you're not fully motivated to do something hard until someone tells you that you *can't* do it. And that "can't" sparks a fire of defiance in you that gives you just the boost you need to rise to the challenge.

Leading in the Waiting

I never set out to run Webex Hologram. In fact, my original proposal for a small tiger team to explore the AR/VR space included an ask that "someone" should run this. I never intended that someone be me. I was working in a strategy capacity—pointing out ideas and focus areas for the business to pay attention to. Not to run them. My intent was to move on to the next idea.

Also, I was eight and a half months pregnant with kid #2 when I made that proposal and went out on maternity leave shortly after. When I came back four months later to check on the progress of the tiger team, I discovered nothing had happened. Other priorities had derailed it, and the leader assigned to run it had been reprioritized to other things. So, I picked it up again. There was still validity in, and support for, the idea, so I led the tiger team to a proposal for action with three possible scenarios: conservative, Go Big!, or an in-between approach.

Our executive team decided they wanted to Go Big! So, I walked away with the action to build a Go Big plan—come up with the team, money, and resources needed to move this forward. As a result, our future CTO in this space was assigned as the tech lead to help me develop the technical milestones to execute this Go Big plan. Game back on.

Fortune Favors the Bold

As the tech lead and I worked on the proposal we would take back to our leadership team, the question that was still unanswered was: *Who's going to lead this?* We had unsuccessfully tapped a senior director to lead the tiger team, and discussions had been had that at least that level, or probably a VP level, would be needed to run the project team.

I was merely a senior manager at the time, three levels below what our executive team was looking for. But no leader could be found, and at this point, I had been driving this effort forward for over a year and becoming clearer on the path I wanted to see carved forward. So when we proposed our project plan and team, I put my name in as the project lead. Maybe it was a little bit of that defiance I felt back from my college years, thinking again the answer would be "no." Maybe I was channeling a bit of Ayn Rand's spirit in *The Fountainhead* often paraphrased as: "The question isn't who is going to let me; it's who is going to stop me?" In this case my boss endorsed me, and our SVP signed off, and the rest, as they say, is history. In this case I didn't even have to verbally hear that "no." It was simply the fear of it that rallied a defiant determination in me to strive for "yes."

22

Find Your Huckleberry

"I want to hear more about Sam. Frodo
wouldn't have got far without Sam."

—FRODO, *THE TWO TOWERS* (2002 SCREEN ADAPTATION)

While trailblazing might dictate the necessity of making some hard steps alone, being an out-front leader doesn't mean being devoid of all friendships, alliances, and support; in fact, quite the contrary. Having the right partner(s) to help you on the journey can make all the difference. Up to this point in my career, I had been the classic "intrapreneur" and tended to look at every project team as if it were my start-up.

As any start-up founder will tell you, finding advisors and confidantes who can help you is very important, but it is also crucial to find those one or two special people who round out your skill sets, are strong where you are weak, and can act as an extension of yourself when you need to run fast.

My Huckleberry

Nearly a decade ago, I met Ashley. She was instrumental in this project, and her name has popped up more than once on the preceding pages. When we first met, she was underutilized in an adjacent group while I was drowning with too much on my plate in a strategic alliances role. Ashley was assigned to me on a part-time loan to fill her plate and free up mine. It worked beautifully on both sides. After a year or so of indirectly working together, Ashley was transferred to my team full-time, and she hasn't left my side since. She is my Sam.

In the 1993 version of *Tombstone*, Val Kilmer portrays an iconic Doc Holliday who utters the famous line: "I'm your huckleberry." The origins of this phrase are a bit unknown, with some tracing it back to Arthurian legend when a knight would drape a huckleberry garland over his lance as a symbol of allegiance to a lord or lady.[13] My favorite interpretation of the phrase derives from Mark Twain's Huckleberry Finn as a loyal companion to Tom Sawyer, which embodies the spirit of "name the job and I'll go with you." Over the past several years, fulfilling every sense of that definition, Ashley has been my huckleberry.

Other as Needed

When I first embarked on this project, I led the effort as our "CEO" and worked in close conjunction with our technical mastermind as "CTO" and Ashley as "COO." In her role, we joked that a large portion of her job description fell under "other as needed." Ashley has been my trusted and loyal companion in all my endeavors, continually evolving to meet the new challenges of the task at hand. As part of a development program she took, she once asked me to describe what I felt were her two greatest strengths, to which I responded:

Firstly, she can bring joy to every situation and accurately read people and situations in a way that allows her to build amazingly cohesive and well-tuned teams that will do anything for her. When posed with this same question as part of this review, one of our engineers answered similarly: "You have an uncanny ability to raise the spirits in the room. I, for one, am not always wanting to be raised because I like being a grump sometimes. However, I am never annoyed because I know you are as close to genuine as anyone I know in bringing optimism, excitement, and general fun to a group of people."

The second quality I noted was Ashley's ability to jump in the deep end and learn how to swim on the way. When she doesn't know how to do something, she does it and learns in the doing. In the learning, she's likely to build a how-to guide in case somebody else needs to learn how to do it, and in the process, she quickly goes from novice student to master teacher.

Finding your companion(s) for the journey is essential to making it the long haul. Find your huckleberry. Find that person who will say "name the job and I'll go with you." I, for one, wouldn't have got far without my Sam.

23

Protect Yourself

"If you don't prioritize your life, someone else will."

—GREG MCKEOWN

In protecting your team, your creation, and your culture, don't forget to protect yourself. Think of yourself as a long-term investment. Bank on yourself as the best long-term bet around, and treat yourself accordingly. It is easy to forget or neglect this step, but I beg you not to.

It is essential to keep yourself from burning out or crashing hard. Before your health, your doctor, your significant other, or your family has to intervene, ensure you are doing a health check on yourself physically and mentally. When creating magic, it's easy to forget essential things like sleeping, drinking water, taking breaks, and eating. It's also easy to neglect your mental, emotional, and spiritual health. Check in with yourself, adjust where needed, and make sure you're taking care of *you*.

For me, this manifests as taking time and making space for reflection. And I need to think of these as two separate, but related, intentional actions.

Take Time for Reflection

To truly reflect, you need to dedicate a significant amount of time for it. This means setting aside a specific time in your calendar, and not rushing through it. You should block off enough time—not just fifteen minutes for a quick jog and some deep breaths (although those are important too!) but hours or even a whole day if possible. In some seasons, I have taken my entire Monday for weeks and just blocked it as "Planning" on my calendar. I'd use that day to think—more often with a notebook and paper, sometimes multiple pieces of paper strewn across the floor to create order and find patterns—rather than in front of a screen, which can offer too many distractions.

Giving yourself a gut check and a health review is not something that can be rushed. You need to take the time to really check in with yourself. Be still. Be silent. Reflect and ruminate. Don't undervalue your "gut" feelings. If something seems off, take the time to explore that. Or, in the words of Victor Hugo, "A man is not idle because he is absorbed in thought. There is visible labor and there is invisible labor."

Make Space for Reflection

Protecting oneself is an active task. To take time for reflection, you need to actively take it *away* from something else. This is why I think of this as a two-part pairing of intentional actions, with the second part being: making space.

Nobody can just take Mondays off for the next six weeks without making some deep cuts in what's cluttering up their time. Making space requires reprioritizing all of those demands on your time and moving reflection to the top of that list. There is an opportunity cost to reflecting, prioritizing, and protecting yourself. Do it anyway. Review and evaluate your current activities and focus areas and decide what can be eliminated to make space for reflection. Referring back to Greg McKeown's *Essentialism: The Disciplined Pursuit of Less*, hone in on only what is essential and then *actively remove* the rest. Often, making space can mean physically changing your space as well: go for a walk, recenter in your prayer or meditation closet, stare at the ocean.

Change your environment to get a different perspective. My mom is probably smiling down from heaven in amusement that I keep returning to her original advice from my childhood and maybe only now appreciating the sage wisdom in that simple phrase: "Go outside!"

A Cautionary Note

Taking the time and making space for reflection is different from delaying decision-making. The first is active. It's a set period, such as a day, to disengage from daily activities, enable reflection, and confirm you are mentally, physically, emotionally, and spiritually on track before proceeding. Think of it like a pit stop midrace—long enough to perform the health check and actions needed, but no longer.

The second is passive. Delaying a necessary decision is simply procrastinating from making a hard call. It is a pretty little lie to say that we are just pausing for a bit, putting things in neutral, parking, weighing our options. But beware of getting sucked into needless delay. Inaction is a choice. Make sure your pit stop doesn't become a parking lot.

24

Always Play the Long Game

"But our plans are measured in centuries."

—BENE GESSERIT REVEREND MOTHER,
DUNE (2021 SCREEN ADAPTATION)

Timing Matters

At the beginning of this project, I didn't know that I was embarking on a multiyear adventure. It was apparent, though, that the time for an idea like this was ripe. We embarked on a journey to make remote collaboration better and more human. Years later, the world experienced a global pandemic that pushed remote working to the forefront of employees', companies', and shareholders' minds. What had been an important challenge to solve became *the* challenge to solve.

So be mindful of the ebbs and flows of business needs, but also be open to massive acceleration. To again quote Victor Hugo: "There is one thing stronger than all the armies in the world, and that is an idea whose time has come."

Get Your Head Above the Trees

"'Is there no end to this accursed forest?' said
Thorin. 'Somebody must climb a tree and
have a look round. The only way is to choose
the tallest tree that overhangs the path.'
Of course 'somebody' meant Bilbo."

—J. R. R. TOLKIEN, *THE HOBBIT*

When your head is down for long periods, it is easy to become myopic, or lost, or both. Planning for calculated breaks to get your head above the trees, reevaluating the landscape, and confirming you're still going in the right direction will help your course stay true. In general, both the most successful teams I've been on and the most successful ventures I've run have included regular "above the trees" planning sessions with the leadership team.

For larger team efforts, twice a year seems to work well—once in January for the first half of the year planning, and then again around June (give or take for the school and summer holidays) for revisiting and course correcting the second half of the year plan. For projects, I love a good four- to six-month defined phase with an in-person, three-day offsite to get the team on the same page. Then I like to have a virtual postmortem to wrap up the phase once our milestone has been hit.

For more resources on phased execution and planning templates, visit **www.elizabethbieniek.com**.

Virtual offsites can be a great stopgap in between bigger planning sessions, but if you can swing it, getting together in person and in a fresh, nondistracting location can be an excellent shot of innovation adrenaline for the team. (Note: The phase ends in the preset timeframe, whether or not the milestone was hit. If you miss your milestone, this becomes part of the learnings in your postmortem that you apply to the next phase. Having open-ended, never-ending phases is the death of innovation culture.)

Separate from your collective "head above the trees" activities with your leadership team and your entire team. It's also good to pause and take a pulse check from everyone on your team. Twice a year, I like to meet one-on-one for a "virtual coffee" (or real coffee when possible!) with everyone involved in my project. This is a chance for us 1:1 to get above the trees and get some honest feedback on what's working, what's not, and how we can improve. Surveys and roundtables are good tools as well, but to really get a good sense of how things are going, there is no substitute for a heart-to-heart conversation. If you ask, and you listen, they'll tell you. Especially when the journey is long, make sure you're taking time to pick your head up and look around.

Home in on What's Truly Important

Keep the end in mind. Essentialism is an ongoing effort. Once you define your North Star, you must continually keep it in front of you. When Steve Jobs knew he was nearing the end of his life, he famously said: "Remembering that I'll be dead soon is the most important tool I've ever encountered to help me make the big choices in life. Because almost everything—all external expectations, all pride, all fear of embarrassment or failure—these things just fall away in the face of death, leaving only what is truly important. Remembering that you are going to die is the best way I know to avoid the trap of thinking you have something to lose. You are already naked. There is no reason not to follow your heart." That certainly helps put things into perspective.

When deciding to write this book, I struggled with what angle to take and how to write this story. I couldn't delve into the technology journey behind Webex Hologram without treading into proprietary IP issues. I couldn't share a narrative of the strategy or decision-making processes without again oversharing company politics or executive strategies. When I thought about what is truly important about telling this story, I realized it wasn't really to tell you about all the painstaking nuances of building an intrapreneurial project inside of a big tech company. What I really wanted to do was distill eight years of learnings—the good, the bad, the challenging, the enlightening—into simple key takeaways I learned the hard way but might help you navigate your endeavor a little faster and a little easier. That was my "why," and I hope I've done that.

25

All Experiences Are Useful If You Learn from Them

"When you arise in the morning give thanks for the food and for the joy of living. If you see no reason for giving thanks, the fault lies only in yourself."

—TECUMSEH

If, at this point, you are still reading, thank you for the gift of your time. It is your most precious gift, and I've tried not to waste it. This has been a unique and interesting journey for me, and I am grateful to all who have been a part of it.

For the leaders who believed in me, encouraged me, and took a chance on me. For the team that built this amazing product: those who were there every step of the way and those who came for a season and gave their all while our journeys overlapped. I'm grateful for the cheerleaders who have encouraged me every step of the way from near and far. I'm grateful for the constructive challengers who, like "iron sharpening iron," made the product, the team, the process, and me sharper through this process. I'm grateful for the opportunity to have lived this journey and I'm grateful for the chance to share a bit of it with you.

The Joy of the Puzzle

My path in life may not have gone how I'd planned. It's very easy to second-guess things in hindsight and play the woulda/coulda/shoulda game. However, I try to look at everything as a learning experience, and if I learned something, it was useful. In hindsight, building a start-up inside a big tech company outside of a formalized process can feel like pushing a boulder uphill.

There are times when I ask myself: *Why did I do this?* But at other times this was the best possible learning experience I could have had. The entire project was like a puzzle. And I like puzzles. The goal of a puzzle is to take a bunch of things that don't make sense and might not seem like they work together and figure out how you can look at it differently.

Sometimes, you have to try things a few times to see if they work. Sometimes, you have to turn pieces upside down. Sometimes, you just get stumped for long periods of time and have to have a good long think on it. But once you get a breakthrough and make a connection, everything changes. New connections that you couldn't see before are now possible. Perspective can change, and you can realize you were looking at everything sideways, and if you shift your vantage point a little, it starts to make a lot more sense.

Into the Unknown

I enjoyed the challenge of figuring out the puzzle of how to turn Webex Hologram from an idea into an outcome. I liked not having an instruction manual. I liked having to face each day and each task with a bit of "I wonder what we'll discover today" kind of ambiguity and enthusiasm.

I learned a lot about how large corporations work: how to build winning coalitions across groups, how to sell an idea to a wide variety of audiences, how to be patient and wait for the right timing, how to pick myself up and try for another "yes" after the sixth path in a row led to "no." I like what I learned about leading a team and building a culture I wanted to work in. I met some amazing people along the way, and we have some incredible memories and accomplishments to remember and make us smile.

In this process, I learned so much about people dynamics—how to work with different styles, egos, personalities, fears, ambitions, emotions, and quirks. I learned to realize that things are not always what they seem, and sometimes you have to go through layers and layers to really understand what's at play. I learned leading is a lot like playing chess, solving puzzles, parenting, continuously learning, and cheerleading those around you. I learned I can do hard things on my own, but I can do *amazing* things together with a group of people united toward a single cause. I've learned so much and learned I have so much more to learn. Cheers to the journey!

Your Turn

That's my journey. And I'm working on my next step. But what about you? Innovation isn't a thing; it's a mindset. You can be innovative in your life, your family, your hobbies, your career, your company, and your conversations. What's your next step? *What is that one thing you really want to do but are too scared to try?*

Don't shy away from something amazing just because it's encased in hard work. You can do hard things. Who cares if someone calls you crazy? If somebody *doesn't* call you crazy, you probably aren't thinking big enough. So think long and deep about what really, truly sets your soul on fire. Find your angel, make your plan, keep it simple, make your pitch, find your people, be decisive, communicate clearly, celebrate each step, have that cake on Tuesday, and find joy in the journey while you persist, persist, persist. You only have one life, and it's rushing by day by day. So, dream big. Do big. And for Pete's sake, go outside!

If you've enjoyed these lessons,
continue the journey at **www.elizabethbieniek.com** and
www.linkedin.com/in/elizabethbieniek.

Endnotes

1   Victoria Schwarz and Wilson Pruitt, "Thomas Ken, History of Hymns: 'Praise God, from Whom All Blessings Flow,'" accessed January 12, 2024, https://www.umcdiscipleship.org/articles/history-of-hymns-praise-god-from-whom-all-blessings-flow.

2   Monty Python, "Argument Clinic - Monty Python - The Secret Policeman's Balls," accessed January 4, 2024, https://youtu.be/DkQhK8O9Jik.

3   Greg McKeown, *Essentialism: The Disciplined Pursuit of Less* (New York: Crown, 2014).

4   J. R. R. Tolkien, *The Fellowship of the Ring* (New York: HarperCollins, 1991).

5   Ashley Alexis Hamic, Automatic Adjusting Background. US 11593947B2, 2020.

6   Liz Wiseman, *Multipliers: How the Best Leaders Make Everyone Smarter* (New York: HarperCollins, 2017), 148.

7   Ibid.

8   Charles F. Kiefer and Leonard A. Schlesinger, *Action Trumps Everything* (Duxbury: Black Ink Press, 2010), 66.

9   Cambridge Dictionary, s.v. "empower (v.)," accessed January 3, 2024, https://dictionary.cambridge.org/us/dictionary/english/empower.

10   Nancy Duarte, "Good Leadership Is About Communicating 'Why,'" *Harvard Business Review*, May 6, 2020, https://hbr.org/2020/05/good-leadership-is-about-communicating-why.

11   *Popstar: Never Stop Never Stopping*, directed by Akiva Schaffer and Jorma Taccone (New York: Universal Pictures, 2016).

12   *The Princess Bride*, directed by Rob Reiner (Nelson Entertainment, 1987).

13   "The Surprising Origins of 'I'm Your Huckleberry' and What Exactly the Phrase Means," The Chive, October 11, 2019, https://thechive.com/entertainment/movies/the-surprising-origins-of-im-your-huckleberry-and-what-exactly-the-phrase-means/.

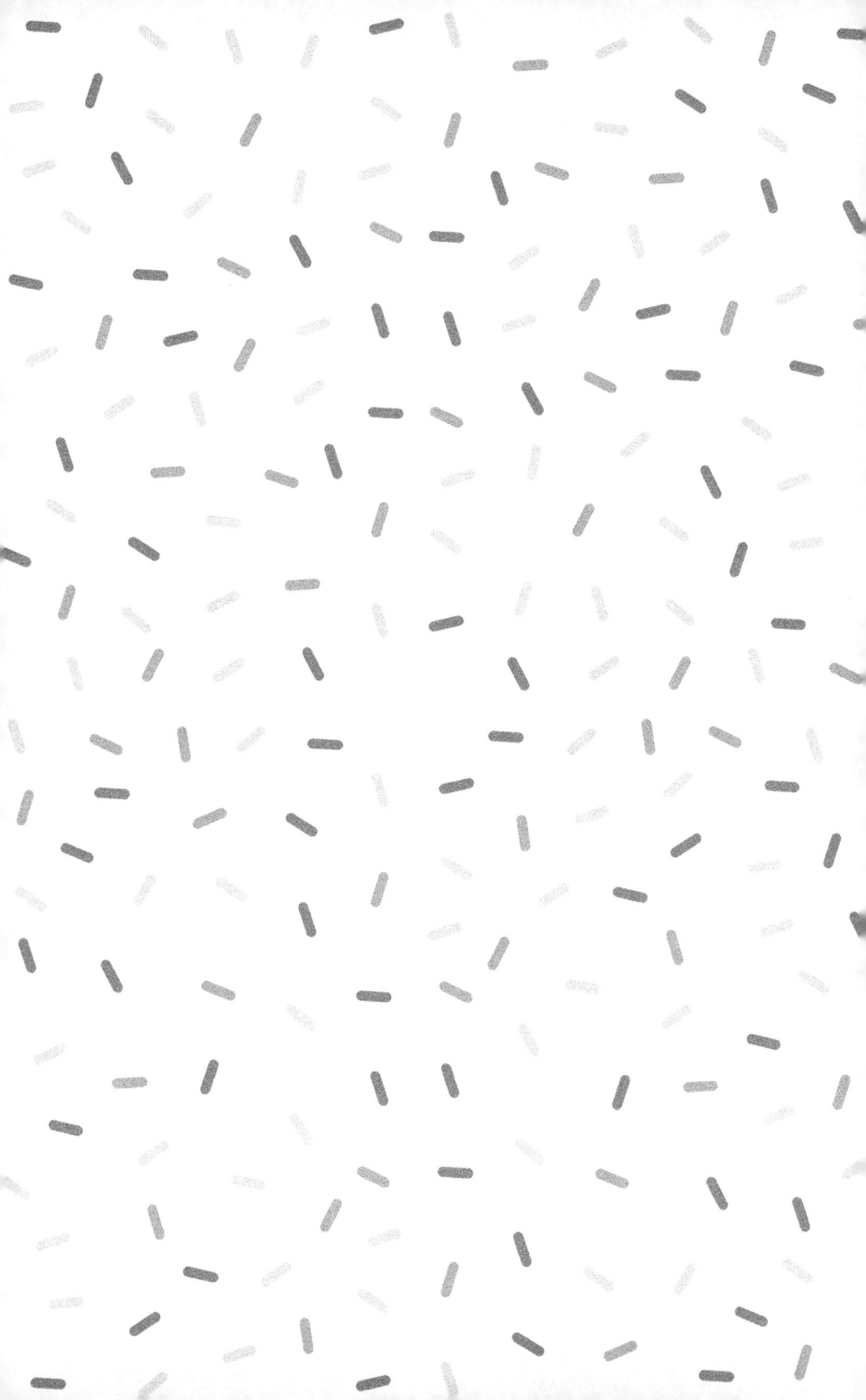

www.ingramcontent.com/pod-product-compliance
Lightning Source LLC
Chambersburg PA
CBHW021931190326
41519CB00009B/986